How to tr
History of Your Car

A Guide to Motor Vehicle Registration
Records in the British Isles

Philip Riden

MERTON PRIORY PRESS

Published by Merton Priory Press Ltd
67 Merthyr Road
Whitchurch
Cardiff CF4 1DD

First published 1991
by Academy Books Ltd

Second edition 1998

Copyright 1991, 1998 Philip Riden

ISBN 1 898937 25 7

The front cover includes a photograph of a Vauxhall Cresta
Estate at Covent Garden Market, London. The registration
number 133 ENM was issued by Bedfordshire County Council
in the summer of 1961.
(The National Motor Museum, Beaulieu)

Printed by
Hillman Printers (Frome) Ltd
Handlemaker Road
Marston Trading Estate
Frome, Somerset
BA11 4RW

Contents

A striking picture of a stunning car! This 3-litre Aston Martin DB2/4 drophead coupé, photographed outside a hotel, probably in the South of France, carries a Middlesex registration issued between October 1953 and September 1954. The allocation books for Middlesex for this period have unfortunately not survived; those up to 1933 are in private hands. *(Gale Canvin Collection)*

Introduction

This book is a fully revised and considerably extended second edition of a guide (first published in 1991) to the main sources available to motoring enthusiasts, local historians and others interested in tracing the history of a motor vehicle used in Great Britain, Ireland, the Isle of Man or Channel Islands since registration began at the beginning of the twentieth century. In particular, it provides full details of where local authority vehicle registration records, the most important single source of information, are now to be found, prefaced by an outline of how registration has developed.

Vehicle registration, using index marks made up of letters and numbers, was introduced in 1903 and was for many years administered by the larger local authorities until the Vehicle and Driving Licences Act of 1969 paved the way for sweeping changes. The registration of vehicles and licensing of drivers was transferred from the local authorities, which since 1920 had acted as agents of the Minister of Transport, to the department itself, which established a single computerised record of both vehicles and drivers in Swansea. In place of nearly two hundred offices previously maintained by local councils, the department retained only some 80 public service points, on the assumption that most motorists, as well as the trade, would in future deal with the Driver and Vehicle Licensing Centre by post or through the Post Office.

Centralisation on this scale clearly had major implications for the survival and preservation of the records kept by over a hundred local authorities since 1903. Unfortunately, the transfer of responsibility, originally intended to be complete by 1 April 1971, extended for another seven years, during which time the local authorities acted as agents for the Department of the Environment. The transitional period thus coincided with the

5

reorganisation of local government in England and Wales in 1972–4, and the parallel changes in Scotland of 1973–5. Large quantities of material, including in some cases the entire contents of a local taxation office, were lost during these years. Since the late 1970s, interest in restoring and running older cars has grown, together with a corresponding interest in their history, for which local authority registration records are an important source. These records have thus become the subject of considerable discussion in the classic car world, especially where owners of cars not included in the DVLA database have sought to have original registration marks restored to vehicles which have been off the road for some years. The value of the records for the history of car-ownership in particular areas or the history of some of the smaller vehicle manufacturers is also now more widely appreciated. Thirdly, the records can prove an extremely useful aid in dating postcards or other photographs which include motor vehicles with legible registration numbers, as an example later in the text illustrates.

An introductory chapter sets out the administrative history of vehicle registration in both Great Britain and Ireland since 1903; describes what records were created by local authorities and outlines what survives today; and mentions some other sources which can be also be used, either in addition to, or instead of, registration records. There then follows a complete list of all index marks used by local authorities in Great Britain and Ireland, with details of surviving records for each mark and where they can be found.

In preparing this second edition, I have again been helped by local record offices in England, Scotland and Wales and the Public Record Office of Northern Ireland in Belfast. For the position in the Republic of Ireland, I am indebted to a number of librarians, archivists and motor taxation officers. Further help has come from the Manx Museum, the Museum of Irish Transport, the Vehicle Registration Officers of Jersey and Guernsey, and the Council of the Isles of Scilly. The Kithead Trust of Droitwich Spa has kindly made available a list of records in its possession and those it has located elsewhere, which has proved a useful check on my own enquiries.

Special thanks are due to the staff of both the main library and the picture library at the National Motor Museum, Beaulieu, for their enthusiastic help with this second edition.

Finally, I am grateful to a number of correspondents (particularly Mr L.H. Newall of Sidmouth, Mr John Cochrane of Liverpool and Mr Graham Bird of London) who wrote following the publication of the first edition, for providing additional information. Further suggestions for revisions to any third edition will be gratefully received, especially news of any previously unlocated registration records, or changes in the whereabouts of material listed here.

Philip Riden

Nene University College
Northampton
May 1998

When it was taken, the main interest of this photograph, probably of a London to Brighton run in the mid 1950s, would have been the 1896 Benz in the foreground, first registered on 21 June 1949 by Kent County Council to Lewis Evans, when its chassis number was given as 116. The other car is a Sunbeam Talbot 10 (chassis no. 41241), first registered by Lancashire County Council on 1 January 1939, and re-registered by Surrey on 31 August 1954. Its last licence expired on 31 January 1964, when its owner was Mr R.A. Bishop of 75 West Farm Avenue, Ashtead. *(Gale Canvin Collection)*

Vehicle Registration Records:
A Brief History

The Motor Car Act of 1903

The registration of motor vehicles, and the licensing of their drivers, was introduced throughout the United Kingdom by the Motor Car Act of 1903. Registration of 'light motors' (weighing less than three tons) was provided for in the Highways Act of 1896, but not implemented; conversely the Locomotives Act of 1898, which dealt with heavier road vehicles, did establish a system of registration and licensing (but not numbering), which was entrusted to local authorities. Despite these precedents, the registration provisions of the 1903 bill, like the rest of the measure, aroused considerable controversy, with complaints that to number private cars was to treat them as though they were hackney carriages or omnibuses. It says much for contemporary views of the likely growth of car ownership that opponents seriously suggested that private cars should carry names, like boats or houses, rather than numbers. An effective system of identification, capable of more or less infinite expansion, was however essential if the other provisions of the 1903 Act and earlier legislation relating to the speed at which vehicles might be driven were to be enforced by the police. It was to assist the police in this task, rather than as a means of raising revenue, that registration, using a system of index marks, was introduced, together with the licensing of drivers (but with no test as to their proficiency).

The Motor Car Act merely established the general principles of registration and licensing; detailed arrangements for England and Wales were set out in the Motor Car (Registration and Licensing) Order issued by the Local Government Board on 19

9

November 1903, accompanied by a circular to local authorities explaining the new measure. Similar instruments were issued by the Scottish and Irish offices for the remainder of the United Kingdom. Both registration and licensing were entrusted to county and county borough councils in England and Ireland (counties and large burghs in Scotland). The local authorities were to open registers in a form prescribed in a schedule to the order for motor cars and motorcycles, with the option of keeping either a single set of books for both or two parallel series. The issue of driving licences was to be registered separately. A fee of 20s. was payable for each motorcar registered and 5s. for each motorcycle; owners were to be supplied with a copy of the entry relating to their vehicle. Changes of ownership, or the permanent export or scrapping of vehicles, was to be noted and, in the latter two cases, a number thus becoming available might be re-allocated to another vehicle.

The registration numbers themselves were to be displayed on plates mounted vertically at the front and rear of motorcars (arrangements were modified somewhat for motorcycles), or might be painted on the vehicles themselves in the same form as a plate. The size and shape of the plate were set out in a schedule to the order, which established the pattern of white letters on a black ground that was to remain familiar for nearly seventy years. The plates were to be illuminated at night, either by reflection or transparency; in practice the first solution came to be universally adopted. Councils were permitted under the order to supply and charge for number plates but few, if any, appear to have done so. Finally, the order also established the 'general identification plate' system, whereby motor dealers might be assigned a number which they could attach temporarily to a vehicle which was being delivered to or collected from a customer. Such 'trade plates', as they have long been known, were to be listed in a separate register and distinctively coloured: the familiar white lettering on a red ground in use today dates from as long ago as 1903.

The numbering system itself set out in the order was kept as simple as possible and was probably envisaged at the time as adequate to meet any foreseeable increase in the number of vehicles on the road. Each registration authority was allocated an index mark consisting of one or two letters. Initially, 24 single-letter marks were introduced (I and Q being omitted to avoid confusion with J and 0), together with two-letter combinations as far down the alphabet as those beginning with F. In addition, special arrangements were made to identify vehicles registered in Scotland, where all marks were to include the letters G, S or V, and Ireland, which was to use I (although only in combination with another letter) and Z. It is characteristic of the attitude of the Local Government Board of the day, as well as that of Walter Long, its president, that no similar concession was made to Wales, which was treated simply as part of England. Had registration been introduced only a few years later, after the election of the Liberal government in 1906, when for the first time the separate identity of Wales began to be recognised officially in numerous ways, it seems likely that index marks including the letter W would have been reserved for the seventeen Welsh registration authorities, which in the event were never accorded special recognition.

Each registration authority was initially allocated a single mark: in England and Wales the marks were allocated by arranging the local authorities in descending order of population according to the 1901 Census, starting with A for London; in Scotland and Ireland the order was simply alphabetical. For some rural counties and small county boroughs this initial provision sufficed right down to the abolition of local authority registration. In other cases, new combinations of letters were issued at intervals by order.

The regulations of 1903 enjoined local authorities to issue registration marks consisting of the index letter (or letters) followed by a number. This was to form a simple series from 1 onwards, although authorities which chose to register cars and motorcycles separately issued two parallel series, with the result that (until the system was changed under the 1920 Roads Act) the same registration mark might be carried by both a car and a motorcycle. An accompanying circular asked local authorities not to issue numbers beyond 999 for any one index mark and offered to allocate a new two-letter mark when a council exhausted its initial block of numbers. In practice, although a number of additional index marks were allocated in the period up to 1920, local authorities issued numbers up to 9999 to provide greater scope for expanding the system.

In general, despite the opposition to vehicle numbering expressed when the 1903 bill was introduced, once it had passed into law the measure appears to have been implemented without difficulty. In any case, the Act made it an offence not to display a number plate in the prescribed manner or to use an unregistered vehicle on the highway except to drive to a registration authority's office. The only problem seems to have arisen with two-letter marks which were construed as offensive. Thus, when BF was allocated to Dorset, local motorists objected and, in December 1904, the Local Government Board was persuaded to issue FX to the county instead, giving owners the option of retaining their BF number or exchanging it for a new one prefaced by FX. BF was not re-used in the 1921 numbering scheme. Similarly, the borough of Northampton objected to being issued with DF and unilaterally adopted NH, which was ratified later in 1904. Some marks allocated centrally were evidently intended (like NH) to relate to the name of the authority concerned. Besides the use of L for London, RD for Reading and KH for Kingston-upon-Hull (among others) appear to fall into this category.

A handful of two-letter combinations were not issued to avoid giving offence. These include WC and (more obscurely to modern eyes) DD (Doctor of Divinity), DT (Delirium Tremens) and ER (the current royal cipher in 1903; GR was not used until 1933). All but the first of these were used by the Ministry of Transport in the 1920s, and no inhibitions were felt about allocating VD to Lanarkshire in 1930. As a consequence of the decision to reserve certain letters for Scottish and Irish local authorities, the combinations GI, IG, II, VI, IV, SI and IS were not issued as such, although some were later used as part of three-letter marks, nor was ZS, although Co. Down was allocated SZ by the Northern Ireland Ministry of Transport.

The Act of 1903 came into effect on 1 January 1904 but, in the order issued the previous November, local authorities were instructed to open vehicle and driving licence registers at once (taking advantage of s. 37 of the Interpretation Act, 1889), since owners were free to apply for registration as soon as the bill became law. In most, if not all, counties, at least in England, there would already have been some vehicles on the road by the autumn of 1903 and so, in most books, the first few pages would have been taken up with the retrospective registration of vehicles which had been in use for some time, rather than cars newly acquired in 1904.

The arrangements made under the 1903 Act continued to operate until just after the First World War, with the growth in car ownership being accommodated by the issue of additional index marks to the larger local authorities, especially the London County Council, which by 1916 had not only exhausted its original allocation of A but had also run through combinations beginning with L as far as LR. In 1906 the system was extended to the Isle of Man by an Act of Tynwald. The index mark MN was issued for Manx vehicles and has remained in use as the sole mark for the island since 1906 (except that MAN is used in preference to AMN in marks containing those three letters). The Channel Islands also introduced registration about the same time. In Jersey the letter J was used, followed by a serial number, and in Guernsey a number alone. (For further details see Appendix 2.) In 1909 the first international convention concerning the passage of motor vehicles between nations was concluded at Paris, which presaged the later use of two-letter index marks beginning with Q in Great Britain for vehicles temporarily imported from abroad; ZZ performed similar duty for vehicles temporarily entering the Irish Free State or Republic of Ireland.

Above: This line-up of cars taking part in a Circuit of Munster meeting in the 1950s is headed by a Fraser Nash, with brown bodywork, first registered by Kildare County Council on 5 April 1934 to Ainslie Halford Verschoyle of Ardreigh House, Athy, Co. Kildare. *Below:* An 803 cc Turner, driven by T.G. Peacock, at a rally control point in Chester. The car, which was blue, was first registered by Cheshire County Council to Brown & Peacock of Three Ways Garage, Clatterbridge, on 25 July 1955. *(Gale Canvin Collection)*

The Roads Act of 1920

The registration system was substantially overhauled by the Roads Act of 1920, the first major measure promoted by the new Ministry of Transport, established under an Act of the previous year in an attempt to place the state's dealings with all forms of transport in the hands of a single department. Thus responsibility for roads, which dominated the work of the Ministry of Transport from its inception, was transferred from the Local Government Board (the rest of whose functions formed the nucleus of the new Ministry of Health), while supervisory and regulatory powers over railways and shipping were acquired from the Board of Trade. The Home Office, of course, retained its responsibility for the police, who, since the turn of the century, had been as much involved in motoring matters as the LGB.

The Roads Act confirmed county, county borough and large burgh councils as registration and licensing authorities for vehicles and their drivers, although the Finance Act of the same year changed the arrangements concerning excise duty on motor vehicles, which was increased in preference to a tax on petrol. One consequence of this was that henceforth the local authorities acted as agents of the Minister of Transport and records created under the Roads Act have thus been deemed 'public records' in the technical sense defined by the Public Records Act of 1958, whereas those kept under the 1903 Act are records of the registration authorities. The 1920 Act, which came into effect on 1 January 1921, applied, like its predecessor, to the whole of the United Kingdom; supervision of the local authorities was somewhat simplified since the Ministry of Transport, unlike the LGB, was a UK department. On the other hand, given the conditions prevailing in 1920, it was thought prudent to include a clause allowing the minister to administer registration and licensing directly in Ireland, if the local authorities were unable or unwilling to act. As far as one can judge from the surviving records, local administration did not break down in Ireland.

As in 1903, detailed arrangements for vehicle registration were contained in an order in council and statutory regulations, issued by the Ministry of Transport in February and March in 1921. These, together with the Act itself, remained the principal legislation until the Vehicles (Excise) Act of 1949 consolidated the law afresh after the Second World War. The registration provisions of the 1903 Act and orders thereunder were repealed (although other parts of the earlier Act remained on the statute book until repealed by the Road Traffic Act of 1930) and vehicles registered under the 1903 Act were deemed to be registered under that of 1920. Two-letter marks continued to be issued as required, although the reservation of G and V for Scotland was abandoned, leaving only S as a wholly distinctive Scottish mark.

By 1932 the scope for further extension of the two-letter, four-figure system was exhausted and from that year local authorities began to use the more familiar three-figure, three-letter marks. Thus, for example, Hampshire, having reached AA 9999, issued numbers preceded by AAA, BAA, CAA and so on, in blocks of 999 in each case. When this device also failed to keep pace with the growth of car ownership after the Second World War, local authorities were instructed to reverse the order of letters and numbers, which provided sufficient capacity to enable the system to continue into the early 1960s. Throughout this period, a number of three-letter combinations that might be deemed offensive were never issued. The practice of adding a suffix letter to six-digit marks was introduced in some registration areas in 1963 and generally the following year. Initially changed on 1 January annually, the suffix letter was later allocated to twelve-month periods beginning on 1 August, at the (far from unanimous) request of the motor trade. By the time local authorities closed their registers and handed over responsibility to DVLC, the suffix letter had reached M or N.

The legislation of 1920 came into operation shortly before the establishment of Northern Ireland under the Government of Ireland Act, 1920, and the slightly later creation of the Irish Free

State. In neither country were arrangements for vehicle registration initially affected, since, under the Government of Ireland Act, all legislation in force in Ireland at the time of the Act's passing remained current until altered by an Act of either the Northern Ireland Parliament or the Dail. Neither made any change to the arrangements of 1920 for some years. As car ownership expanded in Ireland, additional two-letter index marks were drawn from previously unused Z combinations, with local authorities in Northern Ireland using AZ, BZ, CZ etc and those in the Republic ZA, ZB, ZC etc. In practice, only a few of the larger Irish counties and the county boroughs drew on these additional marks, with most of the rural authorities continuing to rely on the I marks originally allocated in 1903 until registration was changed in both parts of Ireland in recent years (see Appendix 1).

Substantial modifications were made to record-keeping under the regulations of 1921. The traditional bound registers were retained (although renamed vehicle allocation books) but were supplemented by a record card for each registration mark and a file for each vehicle. Separate registers ceased to be kept for motorcars and motorcycles (so that it was no longer possible for two vehicles to carry the same mark) but general identification plates were still registered separately, as were imported vehicles assigned Q numbers. The evidence of surviving records indicates that, although the system was supervised by central government, with the local authorities acting as agents of the minister, whose officials issued numerous orders and circulars to local taxation offices, considerable variation developed between local authorities as to how the records were kept. Some offices appear to have relied much more on the registration cards than the registers, in which only a minimum of information was entered, and some simply did not complete the forms as fully as others. In general, the detailed descriptions of individual vehicles, including the colour scheme of the bodywork as well as engine capacity and other more mundane details, will not be found in registers kept under the 1920 Act. On the other hand, the registration cards were supposed to include chassis numbers, a unique identifier which can generally be related to manufacturers' records (where they have survived) and which are an important aid to establishing the history (and in some cases the alleged authenticity, antiquity and value) of particular vehicles.

Under the 1921 regulations, like those of 1903, registration authorities were supposed to keep track of changes in ownership, scrapping or export of vehicles registered in their areas. In practice, information of this sort does not seem to have been entered systematically in the registers, although the cards and files may have been marked accordingly. Subsidiary series of forms used for the notification of movements of vehicles between registration authorities have only occasionally survived to reach local record offices.

The system had also to accommodate the demand for 'cherished numbers' (or 'personal plates'), typically those which contain a minimum of letters or numbers, three-letter marks in which the letters spell a word or form the initials of the owner, or which for some other reason are deemed to be of special interest. Although such numbers are now marketed commercially by the Driver and Vehicle Licensing Agency, in the days of local authority registration they originated simply as marks issued in the ordinary way which were subsequently transferred from one vehicle to another at the request of an owner, in contradistinction to the normal procedure whereby the vehicle retained the same number as it passed from one owner to the next. Because of the extraordinary rise in the value of cherished numbers, allegations of fraudulently compiled plates surfaced in the early 1980s, leading on at least one occasion to Crown Court proceedings in which local authority registers were exhibited. The widespread destruction of such records now makes the detection of fraud of this sort considerably more difficult than it would have been before the setting up of DVLA.

The Vehicle and Driving Licences Act of 1969

The continuing availability of cherished numbers was one of the few aspects of vehicle registration which provoked any discussion when the Vehicle and Driving Licences Bill was introduced into the Commons in November 1968. The bill passed an uneventful second reading one Friday morning, in which few criticisms were made from either side of the House about what was clearly an uncontroversial measure. Indeed, the joint parliamentary secretary to the Ministry of Transport, in moving the second reading, commented on how few representations had been received during the bill's preparation from any part of the extensive and well organised motoring lobby outside Parliament. The minister announced that the number of local taxation offices would be reduced from 189 to 81, although it would still be possible to pay tax at post offices. A single centralised record of both vehicles and their drivers would be established in a development area in need of new office jobs (i.e. at Swansea, in a region then very short of female clerical work), using a (preferably British) computer. At no stage in the debates in either House or in committee was the question of local authority records and their future raised by either ministers or back-bench speakers. The only issue which aroused real anger was typically English: the question of whether or not residents of the Isles of Scilly were liable to pay motor tax to use roads which may or may not have been public highways.

The bill received royal assent in June 1969. In the second reading debate, the minister had expressed the hope that the changeover to a single record would be complete by 1975. In the event, the transitional period extended beyond this and the last agency arrangements between what was by this date the Department of the Environment and local authorities (by now reorganised in both England and Wales and Scotland) were terminated on 31 March 1978.

The Fate of Local Authority Records

What precisely was done with registration records during the lengthy period between 1969 and 1978, or indeed in the following five years up to 1983, when DVLA announced that no further records relating to existing registration marks would be added to their database, remains unclear. In the course of preparing the first edition of this guide, however, I spoke to a number of archivists throughout Great Britain who were in post at the time, virtually all of whom felt that large quantities of records were destroyed unnecessarily. Some of these losses may be ascribed to the general problems of local government reorganisation, especially in county boroughs, where it sometimes proved difficult to safeguard records of any kind. In other cases it is clear that destruction followed the issue by the Department of the Environment in 1977 of an instruction to local offices to destroy all vehicle files which had been inactive for more than twelve months. Nothing was said in this circular about the possible transfer of material to local record offices, except in the case of pre-1920 registers, which taxation offices were recommended to offer to 'their local archivist'. Whilst this may have been a reasonable suggestion in England and Wales, it was less helpful in Scotland, where there were very few local archivists in the mid 1970s.

In the case of vehicle files on which there had been recent activity, the DOE evidently instructed local offices to transfer the material to its new Driver and Vehicle Licensing Centre at Swansea. During the 1970s the department maintained at least two intermediate stores elsewhere in South Wales at Pontypool and Llandow. Since DVLA now hold no local authority registration records at Swansea, and both outstores have been given up, the most obvious conclusion is that, once any information deemed to be needed for current administrative use had been extracted from the records for entry on to the DVLA database, the original records were destroyed. No local repository with registration records appears to have received them from DVLA, although there seem to be some instances in which DVLA returned local authority records to police forces. There may also have been cases where records were transferred directly from local taxation offices to the police: it is now difficult to distinguish one process from the other. Nor is it easy to establish what information was transferred from surrendered local authority records to the Swansea computer, since the main source for the database seems to have been the log books issued to vehicle keepers by local authorities, which the public were required to surrender to the department in exchange for a computer-printed Vehicle Registration Document (Form V5, still familiarly called a 'log book'). At any rate, enquiries received today by DVLA concerning the former 'keeper history' of vehicles registered on their computer are answered by the supply of prints from microfilm of local authority log books; the books themselves have presumably been destroyed.

The first formal action by the Public Record Office concerning the fate of local authority registration records in England and Wales was taken in January 1978, when the department issued a circular to local repositories drawing attention to the availability of the material and its imminent destruction. By 1978, however, it was a little late to write that registration was 'being centralised and computerised at Swansea', since the process was largely complete and many records had been destroyed either locally or in South Wales. The PRO circular distinguished between registers kept under the Motor Car Act of 1903, which were the property of the local authorities which originally kept the registers (or their successors under reorganisation), and records (registers, registration cards and files) kept after 1921, which were public records. A small sample of the second category were to be transferred to the PRO but the remainder had not been judged worthy of permanent preservation. 'However', the letter continued, 'those of the period 1921 to 1939 have some interest from the point of view of local history and the historian of the motor industry', and it was therefore proposed to offer them (as well as the 1903–20 registers) to local offices. No explanation was offered as to why records relating to vehicles registered after 1939 (a far higher proportion of which were still in existence than those listed in earlier records) were not also of historical interest, nor does any thought appear to have been given to the needs of owners of surviving older vehicles. It was certainly not the case that all post-1939 records had been retained for current administrative use by the DOE, since large quantities had clearly been destroyed by 1978.

The PRO invited local repositories to contact taxation offices in their area and take either all or some of the records still at those offices, of which a list was appended to the letter. Formally, any documents acquired in this way would be presented to local repositories under s. 3.6 of the Public Records Act, 1958. The letter concluded by asking local archivists to take action 'as soon as possible, as the Department [of the Environment] wishes to commence the destruction of unwanted records in the very near future'.

There were a number of reasons why the Public Record Office was unable to take action to prevent the loss of registration records until the transfer to DVLA was almost complete. Initially, it took some time after the 1969 Act came into force in 1971 before the status of the post-1920 material as public records was determined. Some further time then elapsed before the PRO and DOE came to the agreement described in the circular of 1978, although the PRO had had informal dealings with interested local record offices, some of which had already acquired registration material. The PRO was in any case unable to issue formal advice to local archivists until it was clear what records the DOE itself required; equally, the issue of the 1978 circular was geared to the closure of local authority taxation departments and could not, from its very nature, be sent until the PRO had obtained from the DOE details of records still at local offices. Once the circular had been issued, the PRO's involvement with the records was very limited. A small representative sample of post-1920 material was taken into the office and added to the class MT 900 (which is not at present available for public inspection) and in 1988 the department secured the Lord Chancellor's authority for the preservation of the post-1939 as well as the earlier records.

Since the 1958 Public Records Act does not in general apply to Scotland, the Scottish Record Office could not directly follow the procedure adopted by the PRO in England and Wales. The SRO did, however, attempt to discover the whereabouts of the pre-1920 records of all the Scottish registration authorities, starting with the Edinburgh licensing office, which in 1978 had recently arranged for the deposit of the Leith Burgh, Midlothian and West Lothian records in Edinburgh City Archives. Over the country as a whole, however, the survey did not bear a great deal of fruit and it appears that most Scottish registration records which reached archival custody did so through local initiative. It is also clear that a great deal of material was destroyed, either in Scotland or after removal to South Wales (the latter operation itself being a breach of the general rule that the Scottish records of central government departments should be kept in Scotland).

Preserving the Records

Most archivists who discovered, on enquiry at local taxation offices, some or all of the records included in the list circulated by the PRO took all available material into custody, whether it dated from before 1921, between 1921 and 1939, or after 1939. Only one office (Gloucestershire) appears to have drawn a random sample of post-1921 registration files in preference to keeping the entire series. Similarly, most archive services have listed the documents acquired from taxation offices in a single sequence, ignoring the distinction drawn by the PRO between registers kept under the 1903 Act and post-1921 material.

The bulk of the registration records now in archival custody, whether in England and Wales or Scotland, appear to have been transferred either as result of the PRO's letter of January 1978 or earlier action by the offices themselves. In some cases, however, further transfers have been made since 1978 from police forces, especially of the registration cards kept under the 1921 regulations, since a number of indexes of this sort appear either to have been transferred from taxation offices to the police or returned from DVLA to local forces. Unfortunately, police custody seems to have led to yet further destruction, mainly in the 1980s.

During the preparation of this first edition of this book, I was supplied by DVLA with an undated list headed 'Record of Location of Obsolete Files retrieved from LTOs'; subsequent conversation with staff at Swansea established that the word 'Files' meant local taxation office records of any kind. For some counties, this list confirms the complete destruction of records for a particular registration authority, while in others the location given is a local authority archive service. For many areas, however, the location is a police establishment, typically an information room or stolen vehicle department. I drew the attention of a number of archivists (in Scotland as well as England and Wales) to entries on this list which suggested that their local police force might still retain registration records worth safeguarding for future transfer, even if they could not be taken into custody immediately. Only in one case (Essex) did enquiries at police establishments yield any previously unknown material; most commonly the response was a reply from an officer regretting that the records in question had been destroyed some years ago.

One other location must also be mentioned, the Kithead Trust, a voluntary organisation with premises in Droitwich Spa that collects records relating to road transport and has close links with the PSV Circle, a bus enthusiasts' club. In February 1978 DVLC issued a circular to local taxation offices, stating that local offices were free to hand over registration records to the PSV Circle, which subsequently acquired a considerable quantity of such material, especially index cards for the period 1921–48. Most of this is now in the possession of the Kithead Trust, although some is in private hands. This was another sorry episode in the saga of what became of the local registration records. Since all documents created under the 1920 Roads Act or later legislation were public records (in the technical sense as defined by the 1958 Public Records Act), only the Lord Chancellor (and not the Department of the Environment) could make arrangements for their disposal. Moreover, the PRO (acting on behalf of the Lord Chancellor) had only the previous month issued guidance concerning the presentation of the same material to offices appointed under the Public Records Act to receive such documents. Records kept under the 1903 Act remained the property of the county, county borough or burgh council by which they were created (or their successors) and, equally, the DOE was not in a position to authorise the gift of such material to third parties.

When it became known, shortly after the publication of the first edition of this book, that the Kithead Trust was in possession of a quantity of registration records, an effort were made by the Public Record Office to secure their return to local authority archive services. This was largely unsuccessful (an illustration of the general weakness of legislative control over records of all kind in the United Kingdom) and thus, in the list that follows this introduction, 'Droitwich Spa' appears as a location for records from numerous parts of the country, as do the names and addresses of several individual members of the PSV Circle. It is possible that the publication of full details of just how much material is in the hands of the Kithead Trust will encourage local authority archivists to make renewed attempts have it transferred to approved repositories.

No evidence has come to light to suggest that other enthusiasts' or owners' clubs are in possession of registration records.

The Surviving Records

Although it is possible that more material may still be found, most surviving local authority registration records in Great Britain appear now to be in appropriate archival custody, apart from the quantity acquired by the Kithead Trust. I have identified nearly one hundred different locations for this material and, inevitably, given the way in which local record keeping operates in Britain, have turned up some oddities which may confuse the searcher. Thus, Rochdale County Borough records are divided between the Lancashire Record Office at Preston and the Greater Manchester Record Office; conversely, some City of Manchester records are at the public library, rather than the record office. For Halifax, some material is at the local library and the remainder at the West Yorkshire Archive Service in Wakefield, where the records of the other former West Riding county boroughs can also be found. These anomalies are simply one aspect of a wider problem unlikely to be resolved until a more carefully worked out system of local record keeping is established in England and Wales. In Scotland there are fewer offices to choose from (and fewer records) but similar complications have already set in. In the Republic of Ireland most records are still in the custody of county council motor taxation offices; those for Northern Ireland are divided between two locations.

A list of surviving records for both Great Britain and Ireland, follows this introduction and the information set out there need not be repeated here. It is worth noting, however, that in both England and Wales records kept by county councils tend to be better preserved than those kept by county boroughs and that for several of the largest conurbations (including Birmingham, Manchester and Liverpool as well as London) little or nothing survives. There appears to be no case where all the records from a county council taxation office have been destroyed, although the only Surrey material is in private hands and much the same is true of Derbyshire; the best preserved archive from a shire county is that for Kent. County borough records have generally survived less well and the outstanding collection in this case is Doncaster's. In Scotland, fewer records of any kind exist but, again, material from the rural counties and smaller burghs tends to have fared better than records kept by Glasgow and Edinburgh.

In most counties, the only material to have reached local archive services are some or all of the registers covering the period from 1903 to the end of local authority registration in the mid 1970s, or the card index kept from 1921 onwards, or both. In a few counties cards were raised after 1921 for vehicles registered under the 1903 Act. Only in a handful of cases have the individual vehicle files reached archival custody and then rarely with any completeness. A number of offices have registers of driving licences issued under the 1903 Act but there is normally nothing of this sort for the post-1921 period. Registers of trade plates survive rather better, although these are presumably of limited interest; only Kent seems to have kept registers of vehicles imported from abroad issued with Q plates. The Kent archive also contains a good range of subsidiary records, including statistical returns and files of Ministry circulars. The equally fine Doncaster records likewise include, besides sets of registers and cards, nearly 500 regulations, circulars and other documents received from the Ministry of Transport from 1927 onwards, when the borough became a registration authority. The Glamorgan Record Office has a similar file from the City of Cardiff taxation office of items issued by the Local Government Board under the 1903 Act, which appears to be a unique survival. Such material is of particular importance since there is no corresponding set of instructions issued to local taxation offices among the Ministry of Transport records transferred to the PRO, much less anything from the Local Government Board, although there are some files on aspects of registration and licensing at Kew, as well as the sample of local records in class MT 900.

Two pictures illustrating the varying value of registration records for the history of relatively modern vehicles. The Dellow shown above, taking part in trials on 8 January 1955 with N.E. Dennison at the wheel, was registered by Buckinghamshire on 31 October the previous year to G.L. Hancock of Aylesbury (chassis no. 555489). By contrast, Essex simply registered the Zodiac below (chassis no. EOTTA 112072) to Ford Motor Co. of Dagenham on 5 November 1954, shortly before it took part in the 1955 Monte Carlo Rally. *(Gale Canvin Collection)*

Using the Records

Arrangements for access to vehicle registration records now in archival custody vary a little across the country. Ever since 1903, public access to information in the registers (although not the registers themselves) has been enshrined in successive statutory orders. Police or Inland Revenue officers were to be supplied with information free of charge; others might obtain the details for a particular registration mark on payment of a fee (originally 1*s*. in 1903), as long as they could show that they had 'reasonable cause for requiring such a copy'. This provision was re-enacted in virtually identical terms in later orders and was obviously based on the assumption that the typical enquirer would be an aggrieved motorist, pedestrian or property owner seeking to identify a driver with a view to bringing legal proceedings. The idea of historical research was not conceived of, either in 1903 or later. Nowadays, however, there are few obstacles to their use in this way.

There are three possible areas of difficulty. First, a number of offices impose a thirty-year closure period on registration records, possibly because this is normal, in the absence of other arrangements, for public records, possibly because this is the current recommendation of the Association of Chief Archivists. On the other hand, since post-1921 records have been presented to offices under s. 3.6 of the 1958 Act they thereby cease to have the status of public records and there is no obvious justification for such a closure period. General custom and practice would argue against the eccentric imposition of a closure period *greater* than thirty years; conversely, it should be stressed that, in the days of local authority registration, the records were accessible (if not generally open) for all periods. It therefore seems questionable whether, in equity, a record office could refuse to supply information from registration records less than thirty years old, if an enquirer showed reasonable cause for requiring the details relating to a particular mark. To refuse access to the same records to someone interested in more general aspects of motoring history would seem purely cussed. An office could, on the other hand, refuse to produce some material, especially an insecure index of loose cards, on the ground that damage or loss might result. Second, some offices charge search-fees based on an hourly rate for replying to enquiries by post and a few charge an admission fee. The West Yorkshire Archive Service, for example, charges £15 for half an hour's work on registration records; at Maidstone the rate is £24 an hour; and at Bedford there is a fee of £5 for searching a single registration number, £20 an hour for longer enquiries. By contrast, Ceredigion Archives, in Aberystwyth, 'are happy to undertake simple and short pieces of research for no fee, just photocopying costs'. The Kithead Trust charges £5 for each registration number about which it receives an enquiry, and a further £10 for a certified copy of a record.

Finally, at least two offices have become apprehensive as to the possible abuse of records in their custody following cases which have come to light concerning the sale of fraudulent cherished numbers. The Dumfries Archive Centre, which has registration records for Dumfriesshire and Kirkudbrightshire (those for Wigtownshire are at Stranraer Museum, with no restriction on access), requires a prior written application stating the object of research and the attestation of two referees before it will produce documents or supply information. This precaution, the archivist freely admits, was taken following a case heard at Liverpool Crown Court in 1985 in which documents from the office were exhibited. Sheffield Archives imposes similar conditions. Here the passage of time has dimmed recollection of the precise reason for requiring a written statement from the searcher as to why he wishes to see registration records (which may be given after arrival in the search-room, rather than in advance), or who originally created the condition, but once again the arrangement probably arose after the cherished number frauds of the 1980s. In fact, anyone proposing to concoct bogus registration marks has no need to choose combinations of letters and numbers whose original issue can be traced in surviving records, since thousands of possibilities, some of considerable commercial value, are readily available incorporating index marks for which all the records have been destroyed, making their authenticity far harder to prove or disprove.

Apart from enquiries from the police or DVLA, and possible undetected visits by purveyors of bogus cherished numbers, most users of registration records in local offices probably fall into one of several fairly obvious categories. The 1903–20 registers offer considerable scope for studies of the history of car-ownership in the period up to the First World War, when motoring was very much a minority pursuit of the rich and most owners whose names and addresses appear in the registers can probably be identified in other sources. Such books also form a major source for the early history of the British motor industry, a period from which relatively few manufacturers' records survive from the numerous small concerns that briefly flourished before the industry was reorganised between the wars. The older records kept under the 1920 Act will also be of value for the general history of the industry, especially for the smaller companies. Family historians have perhaps not yet fully appreciated the value of registration records for tracing car-ownership amongst recent ancestors, while they are possibly the only group likely to find much of interest in the registers of driving licences kept under the 1903 Act.

For the 1950s and 1960s, the major call on the records will probably be from owners of cars made during this period seeking to trace their history, either out of general interest or because they wish to have the original registration mark restored to their vehicle. In December 1983, DVLA closed their database to further retrospective entries and announced that an old car which had been off the road could only be re-registered with its original number if deemed to be of special historical interest, either by virtue of previous ownership or (more justifiably) if it was very rare or represented an important stage in vehicle development. This rule, which was bitterly contested by owners and clubs, led to the re-registration of vehicles with 'age-related' numbers, i.e.

a registration mark which might have been issued by a local authority at about the same time as the vehicle was built but which in practice had not been used. In most cases, this involved using 'spare' numbers from rural counties, especially some of the Scottish authorities, with the result that classic cars could (and to some extent still can) be seen bearing marks originally allocated to (but not used by) such thinly populated areas as Kincardineshire, for which all the registration records have been destroyed. Owners who had devoted much time and money to the restoration of their vehicles understandably resented this loss of authenticity, which occasionally reached absurd proportions, as for example with a former Metropolitan Police Wolseley of the 1950s, immaculately restored but bearing a Kinross registration.

In 1990 DVLA announced a relaxation of this rule and now allow owners to apply for the number originally allocated to a particular vehicle, if they can show what this number was. In the case of owners who had acquired the original local authority log book with a car, this document would presumably be sufficient evidence; in other cases it is less clear what would be acceptable. The best evidence would obviously be an entry from a local authority register, although for many owners such a search would be fruitless, since so many of the records have long been destroyed—at the instigation of DVLA, on the ground that they were no longer of any administrative use. When challenged on this, DVLA merely referred owners to the appropriate owners' club. Indeed, so anxious was the agency to avoid the complexities of this problem that clubs are allowed to charge for preparing applications on behalf of members to DVLA for the restoration of an original number (which becomes non-transferable and remains with the vehicle to which it has been assigned). While most clubs contain a nucleus of members who have spent years investigating the history of a particular marque, possibly with access to manufacturers' records, and may have compiled a register of all known surviving examples, not even the keenest historian will be able to produce a certified extract from a vehicle register if the document has been destroyed. For this reason,

DVLA are prepared to accept other, less conclusive evidence as to the original identity of a particular car.

The other major use for registration records of all periods, although their value in this respect seems not to have been as fully appreciated as it might be, is in identifying vehicles shown in old photographs, either because one wishes to find out more about the vehicles themselves, or to help date a photograph or locate the scene shown. Their usefulness in the first case is obvious enough (and no different from using the records to trace the history of a car that is still in existence); the second is perhaps worth stressing, given the growth of interest in collecting and publishing old photographs. With any image that includes a motor vehicle, it is worth trying to read the registration mark (if necessary by copying and enlarging the original picture), since this can be checked against registration records (where they survive) and more discovered about the vehicle, including its date of registration, which in turn provides the earliest possible date at which the photograph was taken. Even if the registration records do not survive, it is possible in this case to turn to other sources (see below) that will help date the picture, and may yield further information about the vehicle shown. This advice holds good for a photograph of an early car once owned by a family member at the turn of the century, snapshots of family picnics of the 1950s with a car in the background, or postcards of street scenes that include motor vehicles.

It may be worth illustrating this use of registration records with an individual case-study. The postcard reproduced on page 35 appears at first sight to be a fairly unremarkable street scene from a village on the outskirts of Cardiff, and was said to date from about 1920 when it was published in a calendar of old views of Llanishen some years ago. In fact, the presence of a motor car bearing the Monmouthshire registration AX 187 (clearly legible when the picture is enlarged) makes it possible to date the picture more accurately. This number was issued on 17 September 1906 to the Ebbw Vale Steel, Iron & Coal Co. Ltd, then one of the largest industrial concerns in South Wales, for a four-cylinder 30-40 h.p. Daimler, described as having a touring car chassis, on which was built a tonneau body, painted red, picked out with black and white. The car weighed 26 cwt and was registered for trade use—it was presumably bought for a director or senior official of the company.

What gives this story extra interest is that on 22 July 1908 the Ebbw Vale Co. had the original registration cancelled and re-issued for a 42 h.p. Daimler, still painted red, but with a 'Daventry Limousine' body. This was presumably a rebuilt version of the earlier vehicle, rather than a completely new car, but the change makes it possible to date the postcard fairly closely, since the car shown obviously has the body of 1906, not that of 1908.

The history of the car itself can be pursued a little further, for in 1915 the Ebbw Vale Co. sold the vehicle to a garage in Newport (Mon.), who re-registered it as a 'public conveyance'. Since it still only had four seats, it was presumably used as a taxi, rather than an omnibus. The car was still painted red, but was once more described as a 'tourer', indicating that the body had been modified again. Three years later the garage sold AX 187 to the National War Savings Committee in London, 'For Official Use'. The car's Monmouthshire registration was later cancelled, either because the vehicle was scrapped or, more likely, when it was re-registered with the London County Council. The index number AX 187 was re-used by Monmouthshire in July 1920, when it was allocated to a Rolls Royce owned by Frederick Mills of Llwyn-du Court, near Abergavenny, who (coincidentally) was a director of the Ebbw Vale Co. The Daimler's history cannot, it seems, be traced any further, since virtually all the LCC's registration records have been destroyed, nor do any of the records of the National War Savings Committee survive. Equally, nothing more can be discovered from the Ebbw Vale Co.'s records, nor has the garage in Newport left anything behind it. All this serves to emphasise how important registration records of the period before 1920 are for the detailed history of early motor cars.

THE VILLAGE (No 2) LLANISHEN.

3313

ERNEST T. BUSH

At first sight, the postcard above appears to be an unremarkable street scene in a village near Cardiff, with no obvious dating evidence. In fact, once the motorcar coming towards the camera is enlarged so that the registration number become legible, it is possible to establish to within about twelve months when this view was taken and to find out more about the car itself. *(Courtesy Mrs M. Aven)*

Motor Car Acts, 1896 and 1903,
and
Regulations of Local Government Board,
19th November, 1903.

REGISTER O

Index Mark and Number on Identification Plates. (1)	Full Name of Owner, and Postal Address of his usual Residence. (2)	Description or Type of Car. (3)
A X 187	The Ebbw Vale Steel Iron & Coal Co. Ltd. Ebbw Vale R. S. O, Mon.	Daimler, Four cylinder. Th. 30-40 H. P. Chassis. Touring
A. X. 187	The Ebbw Vale Steel Iron & Coal Co. Ltd. Ebbw Vale, R. S. O. Mon.	42 h.p. "Daimler" Limousine body

Index Mark and Number on Identification Plates (1)	Full Name of Owner, and Postal Address of his Usual Residence. (2)	Description or Type of Car. (3)
AX 187	Armstrong Murison Sons, Central Garage, Shaftesbury Street, Newport.	42 h.p. Daimler
A. X. 187.	The National War Savings Committee, (Sir Theodore Chambus, Controller) Salisbury Square London E.C. 4.	42 h.p. Dai

Extracts from Monmouthshire motor vehicle registers tracing the history of AX 187, the Daimler shown on the postcard reproduced on the previous page. *(Courtesy Gwent Record Office)*

MOTOR CARS.

No. in List, 1. Shaw & Sons, Fetter Lane, E.C. (S4376—03)

Type and Colour of Body of Car. (4)	Weight Unladen. (5)	Whether intended for (6)			Date of Registration. (7)	If Cancelled, Date of Cancellation. (8)
		(a) Private Use.	(b) Use for Trade Purposes.	(c) Use as a Public Conveyance.		
nean body, painted picked out with black white.	26 cwt		Yes		17th September 1906.	Cancelled 22/7/08. see page 7-2
inted red, "Daventry imousine".	26 to 27 cwt		Yes		22nd July, 1908	New Regn. See p. 23/1 Transferred p. 12/5.

Type and Colour of Body of Car. (4)	Weight Unladen. (5)	Whether intended for (6)			Date of Registration. (7)	Date of Transfer. (8)	If Cancelled, Date of Cancellation. (9)
		(a) Private Use.	(b) Use for Trade Purposes.	(c) Use as a Public Conveyance.			
eater touring	25 cwt			Yes	27th April 1915.	S. p. 7/2. Transferred 46/6	
eater touring	25 cwt.	Official Use.			9th Dec 1918	S. p 2/5	Cancelled See 46/8.

Tracing the History of a Vehicle: Some Practical Hints

It may be helpful to conclude with a simple guide to tracing the history of a vehicle starting from its registration mark (whether that information is obtained from a plate still attached to the car, an old log-book, a photograph or any other source). In the case of a vehicle whose registration number is not known, the only approach to its history would normally be via the chassis number, about which there is some advice at the end of this section.

The first step is obviously to check the registration mark in the list which follows this introduction, which will supply the name of the local authority to which the mark was allocated. If any records are known to survive, their covering dates will be found in the third column of the table and their present whereabouts in the final column. If there is a dash in the third column and the comment 'Destroyed' or 'Presumed destroyed', that will normally be the end of the matter, unless additional material turns up in the future, although it may be worth using some of the sources listed in the last section of this introduction.

If there are records for the index mark you are interested in, the next step is to contact the location given in the final column, using the list of addresses at the back of the book.

If the location is a local authority record office in England, Scotland or Wales, the best approach is to write or fax (rather than telephone), giving the index mark of the vehicle you are interested in and asking for any details available from their registration records about that mark. Few offices will be able to answer an enquiry on the phone, since the actual records are stored in a strong-room some distance away from the search-room in which staff are located. Some offices will take an enquiry over the phone and offer to ring back; others will definitely not deal with the matter over the phone. As already mentioned, a number of offices charge fees for making searches. Where an entry in either a register or card index is found, an office will supply either a photocopy or a transcript, which can, if needed for an application to DVLA, be certified by the archivist as a true copy.

If you wish to visit a record office to search material in person it is always best to ring first and in the case of the smaller or busier offices more or less essential, since casual callers cannot always be guaranteed a seat. A prior appointment also saves time, since staff can have at least some of the documents you wish to see ready in the search-room when you arrive. Most offices have a leaflet detailing opening hours and other basic arrangements which they will send to new readers in advance of a visit. It is worth mentioning that most record offices (unlike libraries) are open only during office hours Monday to Friday. Some offices use a system of readers' tickets and require searchers to bring some means of identification on a first visit. All record offices can supply photocopies of documents, although not always on the spot: an order may have to be left and the copies sent on. On the other hand, vehicle registers, because of their size, are not really suitable for photocopying, and the office may offer to supply a photograph of a particular entry instead. By no means all offices allow readers to take photographs of documents, and anyone wishing to use their own camera should ask in advance whether this is permitted.

It should perhaps be stressed that a record office differs fundamentally from a library (even a reference library) in that the documents are not kept on the search-room shelves and readers cannot browse through the material. Each item has to be identified from the appropriate list or index and then requisitioned from the strong-room. This takes time, especially on a first visit, and new visitors to an office should be prepared to master the procedure a particular office follows. It is also important to remember that most documents in a record office are unique and irreplaceable and many are fragile. Material must always be handled with great care and notes made only in pencil, not ink.

Although most offices now allow laptop computers to be used in their search-rooms, dictating machines remain unwelcome, since they disturb other readers.

The Kithead Trust ask that enquiries to them be made by letter, rather than telephone, and are accompanied by a stamped addressed envelope, a courtesy that should also be observed when writing to private individuals with records in their possession.

If the registration mark in which you are interested belongs to an Irish local authority, the next step will depend on whether the county or county borough in question lies in Northern Ireland or the Republic. In Northern Ireland, most surviving records have been centralised at Coleraine, as explained in Appendix 1, and enquiries there should be made by letter. In the Republic, most records are still with the local authorities, often their motor taxation departments. Where an address is given in the list which follows this introduction, enquiries should obviously be made (by letter, rather than phone) as indicated. For a few counties it has proved impossible to secure firm details as to what records survive. In these cases, it is probably worth writing to the motor taxation department of the council in the hope that something may turn up. In both Northern Ireland and the Republic, the actual records, prior to the changes described in Appendix 1, are similar to those for British local authorities and their present custodians should be able to supply photocopies.

For Isle of Man and Channel Islands records, the arrangements are set out in Appendix 2. The main point is that Manx records up to 1965 are in archival custody, whereas later material and all Guernsey (but not most Jersey) records are held by administrative departments with no direct public access, Enquirers should therefore apply by letter rather than phone and be prepared to pay statutory search fees.

Two more pictures of cars taking part in the 1955 Monte Carlo Rally, both with Coventry registrations. The 2433 cc Daimler Conquest above was registered on 24 December 1954 (chassis no. D 92695; engine no. 79334); the 3442 cc Mark VII Jaguar was registered on 7 January 1955 (chassis no. 724287 DN; engine no. D 5244/8). *(Gale Canvin Collection)*

Other Sources of Information

In some cases, it may be possible to go from registration records to other material which will provide a fuller history of a particular vehicle.

To take the most obvious case, if the original owner can be identified, it should be possible to trace him in street or trade directories, electoral registers and similar lists of names and addresses available in both libraries and record offices. This may lead to the present whereabouts of the person concerned or his family, who can then be asked for more information. If the vehicle was first registered to a garage, rather than a private owner, it may be possible to trace the firm or its successor. Only exceptionally will sales records have survived but perhaps the principal or one of his longer-serving staff will remember a particular car, especially if it remained locally owned and was maintained by the same garage.

If a vehicle was owned by a company, instead of an individual, it may also be worth tracing the firm (again using directories) and contacting them or any successor. Obviously, the prospects of discovering more about a car will be greater if it was a luxury vehicle bought by a small firm for its managing director than if it was one of thirty bought as a single lot for the sales staff of a much larger concern. Again, it would be surprising if purchase records have survived but, especially in a small company, there may be some personal recollection of a particularly memorable vehicle. In the special case of hearses and other cars used by undertakers, this approach may be particularly profitable, since the vehicles tend to be kept for a long time and, at least until recent years, undertakers were typically small family firms with continuity of ownership.

For vehicles which originally belonged to the armed forces, it may be possible to trace something of their history from service records. Useful starting points in this case may be the National 39/45 Military Vehicle Group (9 Cordelia Way, Rugby, Warwicks. CV22 6JU; tel. 01788 812250) or the Military Vehicle Trust (PO Box 6, Fleet, Hants. GU13 9PE; tel. 01264 392951). A similar approach is possible with other specialist vehicles, such as those supplied to the AA (contact the Group Public Relations Director, Norfolk House, Priestly Road, Basingstoke RG24 9NY; tel. 01256 492927; fax 01256 492599), RAC (The Librarian, RAC, 89 Pall Mall, London SW1Y 5HS; tel. 0171 930 2345; fax 0171 976 1086) or the GPO (Post Office Archives, Freeling House, Mount Pleasant Sorting Office, London EC1A 1BB; tel. 0171 239 2570; fax 0171 239 2576).

If a vehicle is known, either from registration records or other sources, to have been owned by a local authority (including the police, fire or ambulance services) there may be other possibilities. Both the acquisition and disposal of mayoral cars, especially by small boroughs, would normally require committee approval and here it is worth searching the relevant council minutes, which should now be in the local record office. For more mundane vehicles, the chance of finding details in committee minutes are less good, at any rate from the 1950s onwards, when the use of motor transport by local authorities became commonplace. Similarly, council archives are more likely to contain photographs of mayoral cars than dust-carts, although it is always worth asking a record office if they have any illustrative material. Cleveland Archives has a photograph of the first car registered in Middlesbrough, acquired with other material from the local taxation office.

All this advice is based on the assumption that the car whose history one is trying to trace has never been used by anyone more illustrious than a local mayor. If a car has belonged to someone who is generally well known, more may be discovered about it from a variety of published and unpublished sources (most obviously newspapers and magazines) which refer to the person, rather than directly to the car. It is clearly impossible to give detailed advice on this subject here and one of the standard local history textbooks should be consulted (see 'Further Reading', page 53). In the special case of royal cars, it is well known that those owned by the sovereign personally do not carry registration plates, whereas those belonging to other members of the royal family do. All such vehicles, however, are re-registered with a new number and thus a new log book which does not give details of previous ownership, before being disposed of. There are apparently a small number of cars now in private ownership which once belonged to the royal family but this aspect of their history cannot be uncovered directly from registration records.

There is also the possibility of using motor vehicle manufacturers' records in tracing the history of individual cars. Before the First World War, and to a lesser extent between the wars, there were numerous small and medium-sized independent manufacturers in Britain, whose output is now represented by a few surviving examples. Even in the 1950s, there were more separate companies than there are today. On the other hand, it is important to appreciate that large quantities of material have been lost as a result of mergers and takeovers, as well as the simple demise of some businesses. Even where records have survived, it is by no means certain that they will identify individual vehicles.

An excellent guide to manufacturers' records (and other sources) to be found in several different repositories in Coventry has recently been published by Warwick University (see 'Further Reading'), and for other companies it may be worth contacting the Historical Manuscripts Commission (Quality House, Quality Court, Chancery Lane, London WC2A 1HP; tel. 0171 242 1198; fax 0171 831 3550), who have a database of all kinds of business records, from which it is possible to establish whether any particular firm's records have survived and where they are kept. The database can be accessed through the HMC's web-site, which also contains a great deal of other useful information about archives and where to find them.

For vehicles belonging to marques now owned by Rover Group (principally those brought together to become the British Motor Corporation, later British Leyland), the British Motor

Industry Heritage Trust (see page 92) may be able to supply a detailed production record, including colour, date built, date despatched, destination, and any special equipment. Makes covered include Austin, Austin-Healey, Land Rover, Metropolitan, Mini, MG, Morris, Range Rover, Riley, Rover, Standard, Triumph, Vanden Plas Princess and Wolseley, mostly for the period since the Second World War. Similarly, the British Commercial Vehicle Museum at Leyland (see page 93) has an extensive archive and library relating to this aspect of BL's history, including material from other commercial vehicle manufacturers acquired by Leyland after 1945. Likewise, the Sir Henry Royce Memorial Foundation (The Hunt House, Paulerspury, Northants. NN12 7NA; tel. 01327 811048; fax 01327 811797) has the older records of Rolls Royce (and Bentley from 1933), including details of over 100,000 individual cars, as well as a library of printed and photographic material.

With any investigation of this kind into the history of a particular vehicle, the vital starting-point will normally be a chassis number, unique to the car in question, which can, with luck, be matched against factory records. Indeed, in the absence of a registration number, the chassis number is the only obvious reference, since, where they survive, manufacturers' records should then at least provide a date of building and possibly the name of a customer. Ideally, other identifying data, such as the engine number and body number, should also be used to confirm the authenticity of a vehicle or to match it securely against makers' records.

Another major source of information and advice are the owners' clubs and registers which exist for virtually every make of car and, in some cases, individual models or ranges. Anyone tracing the history of a specific car, even if only from a photograph rather than as the owner of a surviving example, would be well advised to contact the appropriate club, whose members will invariably have an expert collective knowledge of the marque, model and possibly individual car concerned. Since most clubs are staffed by voluntary officers, names and addresses change too rapidly for a list to be given here, but the details can be found in the monthly magazine *Practical Classics*. Most clubs produce a magazine of their own, which will probably be happy to publish a 'mystery photograph' of a car and invite readers to identify it (as do some of the commercially produced magazines and the motoring section of the Saturday *Daily Telegraph*). Owners' clubs are also by far the best (and indeed usually the only) source of authoritative advice concerning the genuineness (and thus value) of vehicles, and for this reason their help has been enlisted by DVLA in the preparation of applications for the restoration of original registration numbers.

Most makes of car are also well served by published secondary literature, which will provide a general history of the manufacturer and their products, although not always details of individuals vehicles. A local reference library will have a range of such material covering the more popular makes, as well as the main encylopaedias which seek to list all cars of a certain period, or in one case all cars produced in Britain between 1895 and 1975 (see 'Further Reading', page 53). More obscure titles can be obtained through the inter-library loan service or bought from specialist booksellers. It is also possible to use the library of the National Motor Museum at Beaulieu (Brockenhurst, Hants. SO42 7ZN; tel. 01590 612345; fax 01590 612655), which has the finest collection of printed material relating to the subject, including sales literature, repair manuals and similar items that are not 'publications' in the conventional sense, as well as bound runs of the main motoring magazines. The library is open seven days a week without charge (although donations are appreciated).

Besides Beaulieu there are numerous other motor or transport museums around the country, which are listed at the end of this book. Most should be able to offer some advice about the history of a particular car. More generally, any museum in a town associated with the motor vehicle industry is likely to have information on local manufacturers.

Finally, it is worth mentioning a source of value where registration records do not survive, *Glass's Index of Registration*

Index Marks	Licensing Authority	Month First Issued	1st Serial No. issued in Jan. of intervening years (Years=Bold type: Nos.=Italics)	Month Last Issued
ABD	Northamptonshire	Oct. 37	. 38=378 .	Apr. 38
ABD-B	Northamptonshire	Mar. 64	. . .	Mar. 64
ABE	Lindsey, Lincs.	Aug. 37	. 38=659 .	Mar. 38
ABE-B	Lindsey, Lincs.	June 64	. . .	June 64
ABF	(Staffordshire)	Not allocated		
ABG	Birkenhead	Sep. 49	. 50=216 .	Dec. 50
ABG-B	Birkenhead	Oct. 64	. . .	Dec. 64
ABG-C	Birkenhead	Jan. 65	. 650/on .	1965
ABH	Buckinghamshire	Mar. 33	. . .	Oct. 33
ABH-B	Buckinghamshire	Apr. 64	. . .	Apr. 64
ABI	Monaghan	Mar. 61	. 62=505 .	Aug. 62
ABJ	East Suffolk	Oct. 33	. 34=239 .	July 34
ABJ-B	East Suffolk	July 64	. . .	July 64
ABK	Portsmouth	Nov. 36	. 37=294 .	Apr. 37
ABK-B	Portsmouth	Mar. 64	. ⌐ . .	Apr. 64
ABL	Berkshire	Aug. 36	. . .	Dec. 36
ABL-B	Berkshire	Feb. 64	. . .	Feb. 64
ABM	Bedfordshire	Mar. 36	. . .	May 36
ABM-C	Bedfordshire	Jan. 65	. . .	1965
ABN	Bolton	Apr. 38	. 39=800 .	Feb. 39
ABN-A	Bolton	Dec. 63	. . .	Dec. 63
ABN-B	Bolton	Jan. 64	. . .	Feb. 64
”	”	(200—226 incl. allocated to Bolton Corporation Transport Dept.)		
ABO	Cardiff	Jan. 37	. . .	June 37
ABO-B	Cardiff	Feb. 64	. . .	Feb. 64
ABP	West Sussex	June 34	. . .	Dec. 34
ABP-B	West Sussex	May 64	. . .	May 64
ABR	Sunderland	June 48	. 49=480 .	July 49
ABR-B	Sunderland	Aug. 64	. . .	Oct. 64
ABS-C	Orkney	Jan. 65	. . .	1965
ABT	Yorkshire, E.R.	Mar. 37	. . .	Dec. 37
ABT-B	Yorkshire, E.R.	June 64	. . .	July 64
ABU	Oldham	Feb. 37	. 38=820 .	Mar. 38
ABU-B	Oldham	Aug. 64	. . .	Oct. 64
ABV	Blackburn	Aug. 39	40=301, 41=612, 42=722, 43=854, 44=929 .	Oct. 44
ABV-B	Blackburn	Jan. 64	. . .	Apr. 64
ABW	Oxfordshire	Oct. 38	. 39=161 .	Oct. 39
ABW-A	Oxfordshire	Nov. 63	. . .	Dec. 63
ABW-B	Oxfordshire	Jan. 64	. (450—999) .	Jan. 64
ABX	Carmarthenshire	Mar. 38	. . .	Nov. 38
ABX-B	Carmarthenshire	July 64	. . .	Sep. 64
ABY	Croydon	Sep. 34	. . .	Dec. 34
ABY-C	Croydon	Jan. 65	. . .	1965
ABZ	Down	Not allocated at time of publication		
ACA	Denbighshire	July 36	No records available	Apr. 37
ACA-B	Denbighshire	June 64	. . .	July 64
ACB	Blackburn	Oct. 44	45=033, 46=234 .	Nov. 46
ACB-B	Blackburn	Apr. 64	. . .	June 64
ACC	Caernarvonshire	Feb. 49	. 50=587 .	Aug. 50
ACC-B	Caernarvonshire	Aug. 64	. . .	Nov. 64
ACD	Brighton	May 33	. 34=871 .	Jan. 34
ACD-B	Brighton	July 64	. . .	Aug. 64
ACE	Cambridgeshire	Feb. 34	. . .	Aug. 34
ACE-B	Cambridgeshire	Mar. 64	. . .	Apr. 64

A page from the 1965 edition of *Glass's Index of Registration Numbers*, showing the detailed information given. *(Courtesy Glass's Information Services Ltd)*

Numbers, published by the firm better known for its price guides.
The *Index*, which is not regarded as confidential in the same way
as the price guides, but nonetheless is not widely available
outside the motor trade, originally enabled dealers to confirm the
age of a secondhand car by listing the dates between which each
two- or three-letter index mark was used and, where this
extended over more than one year, the first number issued for
that mark in January each year. Thus, taking the first mark listed
on the extract on page 47, it is possible to establish that Northamptonshire issued ABD 1 in October 1937, that ABD 378 was
the first number issued in January the following year, and that the
last number in the series (ABD 999) was issued in April 1938.
The value of this information when using registration numbers to
date photographs is obvious; for those interested in the history of
an actual car, the *Index* at least supplies the approximate date at
which it was first registered, which may serve as a starting point
for further enquiries.

   Glass's Index was published annually between 1934 and 1965;
early issues included retrospective details back to 1903, but this
information was later curtailed. With the introduction of suffix
letters indicating the year of registration, the books appeared to
become redundant, but the series was revived in 1970 as *The
Index of Suffix Marks* and since 1984 has been entitled *Index of
Registration Marks*. Today, Glass's Information Services collect
data for the book direct from the DVLA computer; until the
1970s it was supplied by local authorities in response to annual
circulars. The firm has preserved most of this correspondence,
which was transferred some years ago to the library of the
National Motor Museum, which also has a run of the printed
books from 1938. The museum will answer queries concerning
registration marks which can be solved from *Glass's Index*; it is
not normally necessary to consult the original returns from local
authorities. In turn, DVLA will accept the *Index* as evidence that
a certain number was issued by a local authority at a given date
in considering applications for the restoration of an original
number to a classic car.

Appendix 1

Vehicle Registration in Ireland since 1921

Since the Roads Act, 1920, came into force shortly before the establishment of Northern Ireland and the Irish Free State, both of whose constitutions provided for the retention of laws enacted by the Imperial Parliament until either the Parliament of Northern Ireland or the Dail decided otherwise, partition did not immediately affect motor vehicle registration in either part of Ireland.

In Northern Ireland, the Roads Act remained the principal statute until the passing of the Vehicles (Excise) Act (NI), 1954, which was in turn replaced by the Vehicles (Excise) Act (NI) 1972, the basis of present-day arrangements. Whereas the 1954 Act merely confirmed existing practice, leaving registration in the hands of the six county councils and two county boroughs (Belfast and Londonderry), that of 1972 removed the administration of the system from the local authorities to the Government of Northern Ireland, a transfer which coincided with a reorganisation of local government in the province that included the abolition of the county councils. The changeover took place on 1 October 1973. As in Great Britain, details of the size, shape, mode of display etc of registration marks are the subject of subsidiary legislation, the current instrument being the Road Vehicles (Registration and Licensing) Regulations (Northern Ireland), 1973.

In principle, all local authority registration records should have passed to the Vehicle Licensing Central Office (County Hall, Castlerock Road, Coleraine BT51 3HS), to whom all enquiries concerning Northern Ireland registration marks should be directed. In practice, some local authority registers are in the Public Record Office of Northern Ireland (66 Balmoral Avenue, Belfast BT9 6NY) or at the Ulster Folk and Transport Museum

49

(Cultra, Holywood BT18 OEU), as detailed in the list of registration marks which follows this introduction.

In the Republic of Ireland (which succeeded the Irish Free State in 1949) registration remains the responsibility of the 26 county councils, plus the four city councils in Dublin, Cork, Limerick and Waterford. The system of registration marks set up by the Acts of 1903 and 1920 remained in use until 1987, when a new scheme was devised incorporating the last two digits of the year in which a vehicle was first registered.

Most registration records are still in the hands of the motor taxation departments of local authorities, although in Dublin and a few other towns some material has been transferred to archival (or library) custody. Details of the whereabouts of the records for all 30 authorities are given in the list below. The replies given by most local authorities indicate that they hold records from whatever date (1903 or later) they first survive up to the present. Those in the Dublin City Archives, however, extend only to 1954, later registers having been transferred to the Department of the Environment at Shannon, Co. Clare, where the information has been entered on computer.

For various years between 1910 and 1925 (and possibly later) a publication known as the *Irish Motor Directory* (later the *Irish Motorists' Directory*) lists the registration numbers, owners and addresses of all mechanically propelled vehicles throughout the 32 counties of Ireland (see page 53).

Appendix 2

Vehicle Registration in the Isle of Man, Channel Islands and Isles of Scilly

Vehicle registration was introduced into the Isle of Man by an Act of Tynwald of 1905, the Highways Act Amendment Act, and the registers begin in January 1906. There have been several later statutes but the system of registration, using MN as the index mark, has not basically altered since its inception. The registers for 1906–64 are in the Manx National Heritage Library, Manx Museum, Douglas, Isle of Man IM1 1LY (tel. 01624 648000; fax 01624 648001); later records are at the Vehicle Licensing Section of the Treasury (Government Offices, Buck's Road, Douglas).

Statutory control of motor vehicles on Guernsey began with a provisional ordinance of 1903, made permanent in 1908, which provided for owners to notify the constables of St Peter Port of the number of vehicles owned and to pay £1 tax per vehicle. In 1913 Guernsey became party to the international convention governing the passage of vehicles abroad and in 1915 a comprehensive law relating to registration, taxation and the licensing of drivers was enacted by the States. This was replaced in 1926 by a law which, with amendments, remains the basis of present-day arrangements. Apart from minor variations for official cars and trade plates, Guernsey's registration system relies simply on a serial number, which had reached 61000 by 1997. Vehicles used on Alderney are registered with a number prefaced by AY.

Registration records for Guernsey and Alderney are in the custody of the Vehicle Registration and Licensing Department of the States Traffic Committee, PO Box 145, Bulwer Avenue, St Sampson's, Guernsey GY1 3HY (tel. 01481 42214; fax 01481 42175). They are not open to the public but, on payment of a fee, the department will supply information if a sufficient reason is given.

Registration on Jersey was introduced in 1915 under a law enacted by the States the previous year and the principal statute in force today dates from 1994. The registration mark consists of the letter J followed by a serial number. Records from 1994 are in the custody of the Driver and Vehicle Standards Department of the States Treasury, La Route de Veulle, La Collete, St Helier Jersey JE1 3UE (tel. 01534 22431; fax 01534 68910). They are not open to the public but again, on payment of a fee, the department will supply information to enquirers if a sufficient reason is given. Only records from 1994, which are on computer, are available; earlier records have been deposited with the States of Jersey Archives Service, The Weighbridge, St Helier, Jersey JE2 3NF (tel. 01534 633303; fax 01534 633301) and are available by appointment.

Motor taxation was introduced into the Isles of Scilly in 1971, when the index mark SCY was allocated to the Council of the Isles of Scilly. The authority, however, has no registration records in its custody: those created in the short period between 1971 and the establishment of DVLC appear to have been sent to Swansea and were presumably destroyed there.

Further Reading

William Plowden, *The Motor Car and Politics, 1896-1970* (Bodley Head, 1971). An excellent general account, with full references and bibliography; almost the only historical study of the Ministry of Transport.

R.G.A. Chesterman, *Laughter in the House. Local Taxation and the Motor Car in Cheshire, 1888–1978* (Cheshire County Council, 1978). A thorough local study (the only one of its kind), prefaced by a good outline of the legislation relating to motor vehicle taxation.

Kitchin's Road Transport Law (ed. James Duckworth, 26th edition, Butterworths, 1988). Chapter 19 sets out the law under the 1969 Act and later legislation.

John Shearman, 'The Archives of Motoring', *Archives*, II (1956), 369–81. A pioneer attempt to describe sources for motoring history, although omitting to mention registration records.

Richard Storey, 'Motor Vehicle Registers', *Archives*, VII (1965), 91–2. The first article to draw attention to the historical interest of registration records.

Richard Storey (ed.), *Nottinghamshire Register of Motor Cars and Motor Cycles, 1903* (Thoroton Society of Nottinghamshire Record Series, XXI (1962), 65–79). The only printed example of a register, although Lincolnshire Archives (see page 85) have recently issued some of their material on CD-ROM.

Baron F. Duckham, 'Early Motor Vehicle Licence Records and the Local Historian', *The Local Historian*, VII (1986–7), 351–7. Illustrates the use of registration records for the history of car ownership before 1920 by a case-study of three rural Welsh counties, but fails to appreciate how much material has been destroyed.

Noel Woodall (ed. Brian Heaton), *Car Numbers* (Car Numbers Galaxy Publications, 1992). A list of over 68,000 cherished numbers currently issued, with details of vehicles and owners, prefaced by a brief explanation by DVLA of the rules concerning the issue and transfer of such numbers. Earlier editions go back to 1962.

Neil A. Parker, *Registration Plates of the World* (Europlate, 1978). Brief account of each country's registration system, although the information is presumably out of date for some countries.

Richard Storey (ed.), *Automotive History Sources in Coventry Archives* (Warwick University, 1996). Excellent guide to manufacturers' and other records in several different repositories in the city most closely associated with the motor industry.

David Culshaw and Peter Horrobin, *The Complete Catalogue of British Cars 1895–1975* (Veloce Publishing, 1997). Revised second edition of an indispensable guide to virtually every make and model built in the British Isles up to the mid 1970s, with a comprehensive list of manufacturers' names and addresses.

Irish Motor Directory and Motor Annual (ed. Henry G. Tempest) (W. Tempest, Dundalgan Press, 1910). Lists the registration numbers, owners and addresses of all mechanically propelled vehicles throughout Ireland. Reissued at various dates until at least 1925, when it was known as the *Irish Motorists' Directory* (ed. J.J. Blake). Copies are available at the Museum of Irish Transport (see page 96). There are appears never to have been an equivalent publication for Great Britain.

Philip Riden, *Local History. A Handbook for Beginners* (B.T. Batsford, Revised reprint, 1989). The most up-to-date introductory textbook for local historians in England and Wales.

W.B. Stephens, *Sources for English Local History* (Cambridge University Press, 1981). The standard general guide to sources of all kinds, with a short section on transport.

Motor Vehicle Index Marks and Surviving Records

This table lists every index mark used in the United Kingdom between 1903 and the end of local authority vehicle licensing in 1974, and in the Republic of Ireland up to 1987, together with the name of the council to which it was allocated. The letter 'B' after the name of a town indicates that it was a county borough (in England, Wales and Ireland) or a large burgh (in Scotland). The two right-hand columns list the covering dates of registration records known to survive for each mark and their present location (full addresses are given on pages 80–89). Where records are divided between different places in the same town, the locations have been distinguished as (e.g.) Manchester A and Manchester B. Pre-1921 records will normally consist of registers; later records may be registers, registration cards or files. The records may not in every case be continuous between the covering dates shown: short gaps of two or three years have not been noted, although longer breaks are indicated.

Index Mark	Registration Authority	Surviving Records Dates	Location
A	London	–	Destroyed
AA	Hampshire	1904–13	Winchester
		1921–48	Droitwich Spa
AB	Worcestershire	1903–21	Worcester
		1921–48	Droitwich Spa
AC	Warwickshire	1903–75	Warwick
AD	Gloucestershire	1903–74	Gloucester
AE	Bristol B	1904–64	Bristol
AF	Cornwall	1903–20	Truro
AG	Ayrshire	–	Presumed destroyed
AH	Norfolk	1904–71	Norwich
		1921–48	Droitwich Spa

AI	Meath	1904–87[1]	Navan
AJ	Yorkshire NR	1903–12	Northallerton
AK	Bradford B	1903–77	Wakefield
AL	Nottinghamshire	1903–55[2]	Nottingham A
		1921–48	Droitwich Spa
AM	Wiltshire	1903–74	Trowbridge
		1903–30	Bristol
		1936–48	Droitwich Spa
AN	West Ham B	–	Presumed destroyed
AO	Cumberland	1903–74	Carlisle
AP	Sussex (East)	1903–74	Lewes
		1921–48	Droitwich Spa
AR	Hertfordshire	1903–77	Hertford
AS	Nairnshire	–	Presumed destroyed
AT	Kingston-upon-Hull B	1904–18	Hull B
		1921–74	Hull A
AU	Nottingham B	1921–48	Droitwich Spa
AV	Aberdeenshire	1921–48	Droitwich Spa
AW	Salop	1921–72	Shrewsbury
AX	Monmouthshire	1904–74	Cwmbran
AY	Leicestershire	1903–22	Leicester
AZ	Belfast B	–	See Appendix 1
B	Lancashire	1921–41	Preston
BA	Salford B	1904–70	Salford
BB	Newcastle-upon-Tyne B	–	Presumed destroyed
BC	Leicester B	1955–74	Leicester
BD	Northamptonshire	1903–78	Northampton
BE	Lincolnshire (Lindsey)	1908–74	Lincoln

[1] Early registers for Co. Meath have not survived, but the motor taxation department of the county council has about 80 per cent of vehicle files, including that for AI 1.

[2] Nottinghamshire Archives Office has the registers for AL covering the years 1903–20, of which entries up to 31 Dec. 1903 were published in *Nottinghamshire Register of Motor Cars and Motor Cycles, 1903* (Thoroton Society Record Series, XXI (1962), 65–79. From 1921 the office has loose registration forms for all the Notts. index marks (AL, NN, RR and VO) but these are by no means complete.

BF	Dorsetshire	1903–04[1]	Dorchester
BG	Birkenhead B	[2]	Warrington
BH	Buckinghamshire	1903–74	Aylesbury
		1921–48	Droitwich Spa
BI	Monaghan	1933–87[3]	Monaghan
BJ	Suffolk (East)	1903–41	Ipswich
BK	Portsmouth B	1921–48	Droitwich Spa
BL	Berkshire	1904–22	Reading
		1927–74	Droitwich Spa
BM	Bedfordshire	1903–64	Bedford
		1921–36	Droitwich Spa
BN	Bolton B	1903–20	Bolton
		1965–74	Bolton
BO	Cardiff B	1922–29	Cardiff A
BP	Sussex (West)	1903–20[4]	Chichester
BR	Sunderland B	1921–33	Durham
		1948–54	Droitwich Spa
BS	Orkney	1904–76	Kirkwall
		1904–60	Droitwich Spa
BT	Yorkshire (ER)	1905–76	Beverley
BU	Oldham B	1903–20	Oldham
		1926–30	Manchester A
BV	Blackburn B	1954–74	Preston
BW	Oxfordshire	1903–74	Oxford

[1] Under the Motor Car Act, 1903, the Local Government Board allocated BF to Dorset. These letters did not find favour with some motorists and representations were made by the Dorset Automobile Association. The county concil applied for a change, which was granted, and by an LGB Order of 27 Dec. 1904 the mark FX was assigned. The order did not require existing marks to be changed but provided that the owner could have the mark FX substitued for BF on giving notice to the council. The last BF registration allotted was BF 162 on 20 Dec. 1904. A total of 42 car owners and 41 motorcyle owners did not change their registration letters but any remaining on the roads on 1 Jan. 1921 were re-registered with FX numbers, since BF was not allocated under the Roads Act, 1920 (information kindly supplied by the Dorset Record Office).

[2] Some registration cards only.

[3] Registers for 1933–55 and 1961 onwards; also registration applications 'from an early date'.

[4] The only registers are for 1903–20, but the record office has a quantity of uncatalogued number issued cards (which contain less information than the registers) covering all three West Sussex marks (BP, PO and PX).

BX	Carmarthenshire	1907–74	Carmarthen
		1921–48	Droitwich Spa
BY	Croydon B	–	Presumed destroyed
BZ	Down	–	See Appendix 1
C	Yorkshire (WR)	[1]	Wakefield
CA	Denbighshire	1903–76	Ruthin
CB	Blackburn B	1954–74	Preston
CC	Caernarvonshire	1904–77	Caernarfon
CD	Brighton B	1904–77	Lewes
		1921–48	Droitwich Spa
CE	Cambridgeshire	1904–77	Cambridge
CF	Suffolk (West)	1927–46	Bury St Edmunds
		1921–48	Droitwich Spa
CG	Hampshire	1931–48	Droitwich Spa
CH	Derby B	1903–47	Matlock
		1921–48	Loughborough
CI	Leix Laoighis	1940–87	Portlaoise
CJ	Herefordshire	1904–74	Hereford
CK	Preston B	1904–81	Preston
CL	Norwich B	1920–71	Norwich
CM	Birkenhead B	[2]	Warrington
CN	Gateshead B	1921–48	Droitwich Spa
CO	Plymouth B	1921–74	Plymouth
CP	Halifax B	1904–11	Halifax
		1921–31	Halifax
		1921–77	Wakefield
CR	Southampton B	1903–74[3]	Southampton
CS	Ayrshire	–	Presumed destroyed
CT	Lincolnshire (Kesteven)	1923–74	Lincoln
CU	South Shields B	1921–48	Droitwich Spa

---

[1] No registers or registration cards, only an incomplete series of vehicle files.

[2] Some registration cards only.

[3] For CR a register 1903–13 and other volumes (not a complete series) to 1919. For TR and OW only the subsidiary application forms for registration (RF(1)), as for later CR numbers. None of the series is complete. There are also registration cards for all three marks from 1921 to 1974.

CV	Cornwall	–	Destroyed
CW	Burnley B	1904–74	Preston
CX	Huddersfield B	1921–77	Wakefield
CY	Swansea B	1921–29	Swansea[1]
		1921–48	Droitwich Spa
CZ	Belfast B	–	See Appendix 1
D	Kent	1903–13	Maidstone
DA	Wolverhampton B	1925–76	Wolverhampton
DB	Stockport B	1932–68	Manchester A
DC	Middlesbrough B	1904–19	Middlesbrough
		1937–47	Middlesbrough
DD	Gloucestershire	1921–74	Gloucester
DE	Pembrokeshire	1903–74	Haverfordwest
		1921–48	Droitwich Spa
DF	Gloucestershire	1921–74	Gloucester
DG	Gloucestershire	1929–74	Gloucester
DH	Walsall B	1904–74	Walsall
DI	Roscommon	1930–87	Roscommon
DJ	St Helens B	1904–20	St Helens
DK	Rochdale B	1919–21	Preston
		1927–75	Manchester A
DL	Isle of Wight	1921–48	Droitwich Spa
DM	Flintshire	1903–36	Hawarden
DN	York B	1904–74	York
DO	Lincolnshire (Holland)	1911–20	Lincoln
		1932–74	Lincoln
DP	Reading B	1921–74	Droitwich Spa
DR	Plymouth B	1926–74	Plymouth
DS	Peeblesshire	–	Presumed destroyed
DT	Doncaster B	1927–74	Doncaster
DU	Coventry B	1921–63	Coventry A
		1949–75	Coventry B
DV	Devonshire	1929–74	Exeter B
		1929–48	Droitwich Spa

[1] The index mark SCY has been used since 1971 for the Isles of Scilly: see Appendix 2.

DW	Newport (Mon.) B	1914–74	Cwmbran
DX	Ipswich B	1904–50	Ipswich
DY	Hastings B	1903–74	Lewes
		1921–74	Polegate
		1927–74	Droitwich Spa
DZ	Antrim	–	See Appendix 1
E	Staffordshire	1920–25	Stafford
		[1]	Droitwich Spa
EA	West Bromwich B	1925–27	Smethwick
EB	Isle of Ely	1903–66	Cambridge
EC	Westmorland	1904–09	Kendal
		1925–74[2]	Kendal
		1921–48	Droitwich Spa
ED	Warrington B	1922–74[3]	Chester A
EE	Grimsby B	1904–74	Grimsby
EF	West Hartlepool B	1903–64	Middlesbrough
EG	Soke of Peterborough	1903–74	Huntingdon
EH	Stoke-on-Trent B	1904–20	Stoke-on-Trent
		1927–60	Stoke-on-Trent
EI	Sligo	1903–21	Sligo A
		1921–87	Sligo B
EJ	Cardiganshire	1903–73	Aberystwyth
EK	Wigan B	1932–78	Leigh
EL	Bournemouth B	1903–77	Dorchester
EM	Bootle B	–	Presumed destroyed
EN	Bury B	1904–75	Manchester A
		1921–48	Droitwich Spa
EO	Barrow-in-Furness B	1904–64	Barrow-in-Furness
EP	Montgomeryshire	1903–74	Llandrindod Wells

[1] Registration cards for E 1000–9999, dates not known.

[2] The Kendal office of the Cumbria Archive Service has only one Westmorland vehicle register as such, containing numbers EC 1 to EC 466 (1904–09), but also has 37 notebooks, deposited by the last manager of the Kendal Motor Taxation Office, registering names and addresses of those issued with EC and JM marks between 1925 and 1974.

[3] Also some cards in the possession of Mr A.R. Phillips, 16 Victoria Avenue, Grappenhall, Warrington WA4 2PD.

ER	Cambridgeshire	1904–74	Cambridge
ES	Perthshire	1909–10	Dundee
		1904–45	Droitwich Spa
ET	Rotherham B	1903–25	Sheffield
		1936–77	Sheffield
EU	Brecknockshire	1903–74	Llandrindod Wells
EV	Essex	1931–74	Chelmsford
		1921–74	Leigh-on-Sea
EW	Huntingdonshire	1921–75	Huntingdon
EX	Great Yarmouth	1921–74	Norwich
EY	Anglesey	1903–74	Llangefni
EZ	Belfast B	–	See Appendix 1
F	Essex	1904–20	Chelmsford
		1957	Chelmsford
FA	Burton-upon-Trent B	1903–22	Burton-upon-Trent
		1921–48	Droitwich Spa
FB	Bath B	[1]	Bristol
FC	Oxford B	1922–74	Oxford
FD	Dudley B	1903–74	Dudley
		1921–48	Droitwich Spa
FE	Lincoln B	1903–74	Lincoln
FF	Merionethshire	1904–74	Dolgellau
FG	Fifeshire	1921–48	Droitwich Spa
FH	Gloucester B	1910–19[2]	Gloucester
FI	Tipperary (NR)	1923–87	Nenagh
FJ	Exeter B	1903–20	Exeter A
		1921–74	Exeter B
		1921–48	Droitwich Spa
FK	Worcester B	1903–74	Worcester
FL	Soke of Peterborough	1903–75	Huntingdon
FM	Chester B	1903–78	Chester B
		1921–48	Droitwich Spa
FN	Canterbury B	1904–29	Canterbury

[1] A few registration cards only.

[2] Also a random sample of registration files for 1957–75.

		1927–74	Droitwich Spa
FO	Radnorshire	1903–74	Llandrindod Wells
FP	Rutlandshire	1903–60	Leicester
FR	Blackpool B	1920–74[1]	Preston
FS	Edinburgh B	1921–48	Droitwich Spa
FT	Tynemouth B	1921–48	Droitwich Spa
FU	Lincolnshire (Lindsey)	1922–74	Lincoln
FV	Blackpool B	1920–74[1]	Preston
FW	Lincolnshire (Lindsey)	1929–74	Lincoln
FX	Dorsetshire	1903–74[2]	Dorchester
FY	Southport B	–	Presumed destroyed
FZ	Belfast B	–	See Appendix 1
G	Glasgow B	1921–48	Droitwich Spa
GA	Glasgow B	1921–48	Droitwich Spa
GB	Glasgow B	1921–48	Droitwich Spa
GC	London	–	Destroyed
GD	Glasgow B	1921–48	Droitwich Spa
GE	Glasgow B	1928–48	Droitwich Spa
GF	London	–	Destroyed
GG	Glasgow B	1930–48	Droitwich Spa
GH	London	–	Destroyed
GJ	London	–	Destroyed
GK	London	–	Destroyed
GL	Bath B	[3]	Bristol
GM	Motherwell & Wishaw B	1921–48	Droitwich Spa
GN	London	–	Destroyed
GO	London	–	Destroyed
GP	London	–	Destroyed
GR	Sunderland B	1948–54	Droitwich Spa
		1955–65	Durham
GS	Perthshire	–	Presumed destroyed
GT	London	–	Destroyed

---

[1] Also some registration cards in the hands of Mr A.R. Phillips, 16 Victoria Avenue, Grappenhall, Warrington WA4 2PD.

[2] See note under BF.

[3] Registration cards only, with many gaps.

GU	London	–	Destroyed
GV	Suffolk (West)	1930–46	Bury St Edmunds
		1921–48	Droitwich Spa
GW	London	–	Destroyed
GX	London	–	Destroyed
GY	London	–	Destroyed
GZ	Belfast B		See Appendix 1
H	Middlesex	–	Destroyed
HA	Smethwick B	–	Presumed destroyed
HB	Merthyr Tydfil	1904–74	Droitwich Spa
HC	Eastbourne	1927–74	Lewes
		1921–74	Polegate
HD	Dewsbury B	1913–77	Wakefield
HE	Barnsley B	1913–76	Sheffield
HF	Wallasey B	1913–15[1]	Birkenhead
HG	Burnley B	1925–74	Preston
HH	Carlisle B	1922–74	Carlisle
		1921–48	Droitwich Spa
HI	Tipperary (SR)	1928–87	Clonmel
HJ	Southend B	1914–46	Southend
		1921–74	Leigh-on-Sea
HK	Essex	1915–74	Chelmsford
		1921–74	Leigh-on-Sea
HL	Wakefield B	1943–76	Wakefield
HM	East Ham B	–	Presumed destroyed
HN	Darlington B	1915–74	Durham
HO	Hampshire	1921	Winchester
		1921–48	Droitwich Spa
HP	Coventry B	1921–63	Coventry A
		1949–75	Coventry B
HR	Wiltshire	1919–74	Trowbridge
		1919–30	Bristol
		1936–48	Droitwich Spa
HS	Renfrewshire	1903–49	Glasgow

[1] Also some registration cards in the hands of Mr A.R. Phillips, 17 Victoria Avenue, Grappenhall, Warrington WA4 2PD.

		1921–48	Droitwich Spa
HT	Bristol B	1904–64	Bristol
HU	Bristol B	1904–64	Bristol
HV	East Ham B	–	Presumed destroyed
HW	Bristol B	1904–64	Bristol
HX	Middlesex	1930–33	Nottingham B
HY	Bristol B	1904–64	Bristol
HZ	Tyrone	–	See Appendix 1
IA	Antrim	1903–20[1]	Holywood
IB	Armagh	1925–27[1]	Belfast
		1952–57	Belfast
IC	Carlow	[2]	Carlow
ID	Cavan	–	Destroyed
IE	Clare	1973–87	Ennis
IF	Cork (County)	1903–50	Cork A
IH	Donegal	1903–87[3]	Letterkenny
IJ	Down	–	See Appendix 1
IK	Dublin (County)	1927–54	Dublin
IL	Fermanagh	–	See Appendix 1
IM	Galway	1920–87	Galway
IN	Kerry	1903–87	Tralee
IO	Kildare	1917–53	Newbridge A
		1954–87	Newbridge B
IP	Kilkenny	1903–87[4]	Kilkenny
IR	Offaly	1904–23	Tullamore
		1945–87[5]	Tullamore

[1] See also Appendix 1.

[2] At the time this book went to press, the county council was moving premises and was unable to supply a starting date for its records.

[3] The first two Donegal registers (1903–11) have been transferred to county library; others at present at the motor taxation department will follow in due course.

[4] In 1998 registration records were being transferred from the motor taxation department to the county library, to which enquiries should be addressed. The records are incomplete prior to 1950 but thereafter well preserved.

[5] Two volumes, covering the years 1904–23 and 1945–46, are at the county library in Tullamore; the motor taxation department of Offaly County Council has later books for 1951–60 and from 1964 onwards.

IT	Leitrim	1950–87	Carrick
IU	Limerick	1903–23	Limerick A
		1904–87	Limerick B
IW	Londonderry	–	See Appendix 1
IX	Longford	[1]	Longford
IY	Louth	1921–87	Dundalk
IZ	Mayo	1904–87	Castlebar
J	Durham (County)	–	Presumed destroyed
JA	Stockport B	1932–68	Manchester A
JB	Berkshire	1927–74	Droitwich Spa
JC	Caernarvonshire	1952–77	Caernarfon
JD	West Ham B	–	Presumed destroyed
JE	Isle of Ely	1933–65	Cambridge
JF	Leicester B	1950–74	Leicester
JG	Canterbury B	1904–29	Canterbury
		1927–74	Droitwich Spa
JH	Hertfordshire	1934–77	Hertford
JI	Tyrone	–	See Appendix 1
JJ	London	–	Destroyed
JK	Eastbourne B	1927–54	Lewes
		1927–74	Polegate
JL	Lincolnshire (Holland)	1904–20	Lincoln
		1932–72	Lincoln
JM	Westmorland	1925–74[2]	Kendal
		1925–48	Droitwich Spa
JN	Southend B	1922–46	Southend
		1921–74	Leigh-on-Sea
JO	Oxford B	1930–74	Oxford
JP	Wigan B	1934–78	Leigh
JR	Northumberland	1904–61	Morpeth
JS	Ross & Cromarty	1974	Inverness
		1921–48	Droitwich Spa
JT	Dorsetshire	1933–75	Dorchester

---

[1] When this book went to press, the Longford records were being microfiched and it was impossible to obtain a starting date for the series.

[2] See note under EC.

JU	Leicestershire	1931–36	Leicester
JV	Grimsby B	1904–74	Grimsby
JW	Wolverhampton B	1925–76	Wolverhampton
JX	Halifax B	1935–57	Halifax
		1933–77	Wakefield
JY	Plymouth B	1932–74	Plymouth
JZ	Down	–	See Appendix 1
K	Liverpool B	–	Presumed destroyed
KA	Liverpool B	–	Presumed destroyed
KB	Liverpool B	–	Presumed destroyed
KC	Liverpool B	–	Presumed destroyed
KD	Liverpool B	–	Presumed destroyed
KE	Kent	1920–74	Maidstone
KF	Liverpool B	–	Presumed destroyed
KG	Cardiff B	1930–37	Cardiff A
KH	Kingston-upon-Hull B	1925–74	Hull A
KI	Waterford	1920–87	Dungarvan
KJ	Kent	1931–74	Maidstone
KK	Kent	1922–74	Maidstone
KL	Kent	1924–74	Maidstone
KM	Kent	1925–74	Maidstone
KN	Kent	1917–74	Maidstone
KO	Kent	1927–74	Maidstone
KP	Kent	1928–74	Maidstone
KR	Kent	1929–74	Maidstone
KS	Roxburghshire	1903–37	Hawick
		1921–48	Droitwich Spa
KT	Kent	1913–74	Maidstone
KU	Bradford B	1921–77	Wakefield
KV	Coventry B	1921–63	Coventry A
		1949–75	Coventry B
KW	Bradford B	1921–77	Wakefield
KX	Buckinghamshire	1927–74	Aylesbury
		1927–48	Droitwich Spa
KY	Bradford B	1921–77	Wakefield
KZ	Antrim	–	See Appendix 1

L	Glamorganshire	1903–20	Cardiff A
LA	London	–	Destroyed
LB	London	–	Destroyed
LC	London	–	Destroyed
LD	London	–	Destroyed
LE	London	–	Destroyed
LF	London	–	Destroyed
LG	Cheshire	1928–74	Chester A
LH	London	–	Destroyed
LI	Westmeath	[1]	
LJ	Bournemouth B	1929–77	Dorchester
LK	London	–	Destroyed
LL	London	–	Destroyed
LM	London	–	Destroyed
LN	London	–	Destroyed
LO	London	–	Destroyed
LP	London	–	Destroyed
LR	London	–	Destroyed
LS	Selkirkshire	–	Presumed destroyed
LT	London	1917–19[2]	London
LU	London	–	Destroyed
LV	Liverpool B	–	Presumed destroyed
LW	London	–	Destroyed
LX	London	–	Destroyed
LY	London	–	Destroyed
LZ	Armagh	–	See Appendix 1
M	Cheshire	1903–19	Chester A
MA	Cheshire	1919–74	Chester A

[1] Westmeath County Library, Dublin Road, Mullingar, Co. Westmeath, has a volume of driving licences for 1904–12. There may be other material among the county council records at County Buildings, Mullingar, but these have yet to be sorted and listed.

[2] London Metropolitan Archives have only a single LCC register, covering index marks LT 4001 to LT 4400, issued during the period shown above. The only item in archival custody for Middlesex (also at LMA) is a register for 1916–19 for Edgware, Kingsbury, Little Stanmore, Great Stanmore, Finchley, Hendon, Wembley and Willesden. This appears to be a register of car owers, rather than index numbers, and the index marks are highly varied. The rest of the London records have been destroyed; some Middlesex material is in private hands (see under MC–MY).

MB	Cheshire	1922–74	Chester A
MC	Middlesex	1921–33	Nottingham B
MD	Middlesex	1921–33	Nottingham B
ME	Middlesex	1921–33	Nottingham B
MF	Middlesex	1921–33	Nottingham B
MG	Middlesex	–	Destroyed
MH	Middlesex	1921–33	Nottingham B
MI	Wexford	1921–87[1]	Wexford
MJ	Bedfordshire	1932–64	Bedford
		1932–36	Droitwich Spa
MK	Middlesex	–	Destroyed
ML	Middlesex	–	Destroyed
MM	Middlesex	–	Destroyed
MN	Isle of Man	1906–	See Appendix 2
MO	Berkshire	1922–24	Reading
		1935–74	Droitwich Spa
MP	Middlesex	1921–33	Nottingham B
MR	Wiltshire	1924–74	Trowbridge
		1924–30	Bristol
		1936–48	Droitwich Spa
MS	Stirlingshire	1903–20	Stirling
MT	Middlesex	–	Destroyed
MU	Middlesex	–	Destroyed
MV	Middlesex	–	Destroyed
MW	Wiltshire	1927–74	Trowbridge
		1927–30	Bristol
		1937–48	Droitwich Spa
MX	Middlesex	1921–33	Nottingham B
MY	Middlesex	1929–33	Nottingham B
MZ	Belfast B	–	See Appendix 1
N	Manchester B	–	Presumed destroyed
NA	Manchester B	1968–74	Manchester B
NB	Manchester B	1968–74	Manchester B
NC	Manchester B	1968–74	Manchester B

[1] Registration forms only before 1960, fuller information from that date.

ND	Manchester B	1968–74	Manchester B
NE	Manchester B	1968–74	Manchester B
NF	Manchester B	1968–74	Manchester B
NG	Norfolk	1920–71	Norwich
		1930–48	Droitwich Spa
NH	Northampton B	1924–78	Northampton
NI	Wicklow	1922–87	Wicklow
NJ	Sussex (East)	1933–76	Lewes
		1933–48	Droitwich Spa
NK	Hertfordshire	1934–77	Hertford
NL	Northumberland	1904–61	Morpeth
NM	Bedfordshire	1920–64	Bedford
NN	Nottinghamshire	1921–55	Nottingham A
		1921–48	Droitwich Spa
NO	Essex	1921–74	Chelmsford
		1921–74	Leigh-on-Sea
NP	Worcestershire	1921–27	Worcester
		1921–48	Droitwich Spa
NR	Leicestershire	1921–27	Leicester
NS	Sutherlandshire	1904–26	Inverness
		1921–48	Droitwich Spa
NT	Salop	1921–72	Shrewsbury
NU	Derbyshire	1934–44	Loughborough
NV	Northamptonshire	1924–78	Northampton
NW	Leeds B	1921–77	Wakefield
NX	Warwickshire	1921–75	Warwick
NY	Glamorganshire	1924–64	Cardiff B
NZ	Londonderry	–	See Appendix 1
O	Birmingham B	–	Destroyed
OA	Birmingham B	–	Destroyed
OB	Birmingham B	–	Destroyed
OC	Birmingham B	–	Destroyed
OD	Devonshire	1931–74	Exeter B
		1931–48	Droitwich Spa
OE	Birmingham B	–	Destroyed
OF	Birmingham B	–	Destroyed
OG	Birmingham B	–	Destroyed

OH	Birmingham B	–	Destroyed
OI	Belfast B	–	See Appendix 1
OJ	Birmingham B	–	Destroyed
OK	Birmingham B	–	Destroyed
OL	Birmingham B	–	Destroyed
OM	Birmingham B	–	Destroyed
ON	Birmingham B	–	Destroyed
OO	Essex	1961–74	Chelmsford
		1921–74	Leigh-on-Sea
OP	Birmingham B	–	Destroyed
OR	Hampshire	1904–26	Winchester
		1921–48	Droitwich Spa
OS	Wigtownshire	1904–22	Stranraer
OT	Hampshire	1925–28	Winchester
		1921–48	Droitwich Spa
OU	Hampshire	1928–31	Winchester
		1921–48	Droitwich Spa
OV	Birmingham B	–	Destroyed
OW	Southampton B	1931–74[1]	Southampton
OX	Birmingham B	–	Destroyed
OY	Croydon B	–	Destroyed
OZ	Belfast B	–	See Appendix 1
P	Surrey	1921–45	Droitwich Spa
PA	Surrey	1921–45	Droitwich Spa
PB	Surrey	1921–45	Droitwich Spa
PC	Surrey	1921–45	Droitwich Spa
PD	Surrey	1921–45	Droitwich Spa
PE	Surrey	1921–45	Droitwich Spa
PF	Surrey	1921–45	Droitwich Spa
PG	Surrey	1929–45	Droitwich Spa
PH	Surrey	1921–45	Droitwich Spa
PI	Cork B	1937–65	Cork A
		1965–87	Cork B
PJ	Surrey	1931–45	Droitwich Spa

[1] See note under CR.

PK	Surrey	1928–45	Droitwich Spa
PL	Surrey	1930–45	Droitwich Spa
PM	Sussex (East)	1923–76	Lewes
		1923–48	Droitwich Spa
PN	Sussex (East)	1927–74	Lewes
		1927–48	Droitwich Spa
PO	Sussex (West)	[1]	Chichester
PP	Buckinghamshire	1927–74	Aylesbury
		1921–48	Droitwich Spa
PR	Dorsetshire	1923–75	Dorchester
PS	Shetland/Zetland	1904–72	Lerwick
PT	Durham (County)	1922–81	Durham
		1922–49	Droitwich Spa
PU	Essex	1921–76	Chelmsford
		1921–76	Leigh-on-Sea
PV	Ipswich B	1904–50	Ipswich
PW	Norfolk	1927–71	Norwich
		1921–48	Droitwich Spa
PX	Sussex (West)	[1]	Chichester
PY	Yorkshire (NR)	–	Presumed destroyed
PZ	Belfast B	–	See Appendix 1
R	Derbyshire	1905–06[2]	Matlock
		1903–44	Loughborough
RA	Derbyshire	1926–44	Loughborough
RB	Derbyshire	1929–44	Loughborough
RC	Derby B	1933–47	Matlock
		1931–48	Droitwich Spa
RD	Reading B	1928–74	Droitwich Spa
RE	Staffordshire	1921–47	Stafford
RF	Staffordshire	1925–38	Stafford
		1925–46	Droitwich Spa
RG	Aberdeen B	1921–48	Droitwich Spa

[1] See note under BP.

[2] The only records in archival custody are a register of fees for local taxation licences (1909–10), which does not give details of registration numbers, and a series of receipt books for fees (1903–06), one of which (for 1905–06) does include vehicle details.

RH	Kingston-upon-Hull B	1929–74	Hull A
RI	Dublin B	1927–54	Dublin
RJ	Salford B	1931–69	Salford
RK	Croydon B	–	Presumed destroyed
RL	Cornwall	–	Destroyed
RM	Cumberland	1924–74	Carlisle
RN	Preston B	1934–81	Preston
RO	Hertfordshire	1934–77	Hertford
RP	Northamptonshire	1924–78	Northampton
RR	Nottinghamshire	1921–55[1]	Nottingham A
		1921–48	Droitwich Spa
RS	Aberdeen B	–	Presumed destroyed
RT	Suffolk (East)	1924–44	Ipswich
RU	Bournemouth B	1926–76	Dorchester
RV	Portsmouth B	1931–48	Droitwich Spa
RW	Coventry B	1924–63	Coventry A
		1949–75	Coventry B
RX	Berkshire	1927–74	Droitwich Spa
RY	Leicester B	1963–74	Leicester
RZ	Antrim	–	See Appendix 1
S	Edinburgh B	1921–48	Droitwich Spa
SA	Aberdeenshire	1921–48	Droitwich Spa
SB	Argyllshire	1903–20	Lochgilphead
		1921–48	Droitwich Spa
SC	Edinburgh B	1921–48	Droitwich Spa
SD	Ayrshire	–	Presumed destroyed
SE	Banffshire	1903–38	Elgin
SF	Edinburgh B	1921–48	Droitwich Spa
SG	Edinburgh B	1921–48	Droitwich Spa
SH	Berwickshire	1903–46	Droitwich Spa
SJ	Buteshire	1903–31	Glasgow
SK	Caithness-shire	1921–48[2]	Droitwich Spa
SL	Clackmannanshire	–	Presumed destroyed

[1] See note under AL.

[2] Registration cards at Droitwich Spa; original registers believed to be in private hands (enquiries to the archivist at Inverness).

SM	Dumfriesshire	1903–70[1]	Dumfries
		1921–48	Droitwich Spa
SN	Dunbartonshire	1921–48	Droitwich Spa
SO	Morayshire	1903–46	Elgin
SP	Fifeshire	1921–48	Droitwich Spa
SR	Angus	1903–74	Dundee
		1921–48	Droitwich Spa
SS	East Lothian	1921–48	Droitwich Spa
ST	Inverness-shire	1903–75	Inverness
		1921–48	Droitwich Spa
SU	Kincardineshire	1921–48	Droitwich Spa
SV	Kinross-shire	1904–53	Dundee
SW	Kircudbrightshire	1903–76[1]	Dumfries
SX	Linlithgow/West Lothian	1904–21	Edinburgh
		1934–58	Edinburgh
		1921–48	Droitwich Spa
SY	Midlothian	1949–52	Edinburgh
SZ	Down	–	See Appendix 1
T	Devonshire	1903–20	Exeter A
TA	Devonshire	1920-22	Exeter A
		1922–74	Exeter B
		1921–48	Droitwich Spa
TB	Lancashire	1921–81	Preston
TC	Lancashire	1921–81	Preston
TD	Lancashire	1921–81	Preston
TE	Lancashire	1921–81	Preston
TF	Lancashire	1921–81	Preston
TG	Glamorganshire	1930–64	Cardiff B
TH	Carmarthenshire	1929–74	Carmarthen
		1929–48	Droitwich Spa
TI	Limerick B	1904–22	Limerick A
		1951–54	Limerick A
		1955–87	Limerick B
TJ	Lancashire	1921–81	Preston

[1] The Dumfries Archives Centre requires prior written application to use these records, together with the completion of a form attested by two referees.

TK	Dorsetshire	1927–71	Dorchester
TL	Lincolnshire (Kesteven)	1928–74	Lincoln
TM	Bedfordshire	1927–62	Bedford
TN	Newcastle-upon-Tyne B	1921–48	Droitwich Spa
TO	Nottingham B	1924–48	Droitwich Spa
TP	Portsmouth B	1924–48	Droitwich Spa
TR	Southampton B	1925–74[1]	Southampton
TS	Dundee B	1904–81	Dundee
		1921–48	Droitwich Spa
TT	Devonshire	1934–74	Exeter B
		1934–48	Droitwich Spa
TU	Cheshire	1925–45	Chester A
TV	Nottingham B	1929–48	Droitwich Spa
TW	Essex	1925–74	Chelmsford
		1925–74	Leigh-on-Sea
TX	Glamorganshire	1926–64	Cardiff B
TY	Northumberland	1904–61	Morpeth
TZ	Belfast B	–	See Appendix 1
U	Leeds B	1921–77	Wakefield
UA	Leeds B	1921–77	Wakefield
UB	Leeds B	1921–77	Wakefield
UC	London	–	Destroyed
UD	Oxfordshire	1927–74	Oxford
UE	Warwickshire	1925–75	Warwick
UF	Brighton B	1925–78	Lewes
		1925–48	Droitwich Spa
UG	Leeds B	1932–46	Wakefield
UH	Cardiff B	1925–37	Cardiff A
UI	Londonderry B	–	See Appendix 1
UJ	Salop	1921–72	Shrewsbury
UK	Wolverhampton B	1925–76	Wolverhampton
UL	London	–	Destroyed
UM	Leeds B	1921–77	Wakefield
UN	Denbighshire	1921–76	Ruthin

[1] See note under CR.

UO	Devonshire	1926–74	Exeter B
		1926–48	Droitwich Spa
UP	Durham (County)	1927–80	Durham
		1927–49	Droitwich Spa
UR	Hertfordshire	1934–77	Hertford
US	Glasgow B	1933–48	Droitwich Spa
UT	Leicestershire	1927–32	Leicester
UU	London	–	Destroyed
UV	London	–	Destroyed
UW	London	–	Destroyed
UX	Salop	1921–72	Shrewsbury
UY	Worcestershire	1926–31	Worcester
		1926–48	Droitwich Spa
UZ	Belfast B	–	See Appendix 1
V	Lanarkshire	–	Presumed destroyed
VA	Lanarkshire	1922–48	Droitwich Spa
VB	Croydon B	–	Presumed destroyed
VC	Coventry B	1929–63	Coventry A
		1949–75	Coventry B
VD	Lanarkshire	1930–48	Droitwich Spa
VE	Cambridgeshire	1928–77	Cambridge
VF	Norfolk	1930–71	Norwich
		1927–48	Droitwich Spa
VH	Huddersfield B	1921–77	Wakefield
VJ	Herefordshire	1921–74	Hereford
VK	Necastle-upon-Tyne B	–	Presumed destroyed
VL	Lincoln B	1928–74	Lincoln
VM	Manchester B	1968–74	Manchester B
VN	Yorkshire (NR)	–	Presumed destroyed
VO	Nottinghamshire	1928–55[1]	Nottingham A
		1928–48	Droitwich Spa
VP	Birmingham B	–	Destroyed
VR	Manchester B	1968–74	Manchester B
VS	Greenock B	1921–48	Droitwich Spa

[1] See note under AL.

VT	Stoke-on-Trent B	1904–20	Stoke-on-Trent
		1927–60	Stoke-on-Trent
VU	Manchester B	1968–74	Manchester B
VV	Northampton B	1930–78	Northampton
VW	Essex	1927–74	Chelmsford
		1927–74	Leigh-on-Sea
VX	Essex	1929–74	Chelmsford
		1921–74	Leigh-on-Sea
VY	York B	1928–74	York
VZ	Tyrone	–	See Appendix 1
W	Sheffield B	1903–05	Sheffield
WA	Sheffield B	1931–77	Sheffield
WB	Sheffield B	1931–77	Sheffield
WC	Essex	1962–74	Chelmsford
		1962–74	Leigh-on-Sea
WD	Warwickshire	1930–75	Warwick
WE	Sheffield B	1931–77	Sheffield
WF	Yorkshire (ER)	1932–76	Beverley
WG	Stirlingshire	–	Presumed destroyed
WH	Bolton	1965–74	Bolton
WI	Waterford B	1930–87	Waterford
WH	Sheffield B	1931–77	Sheffield
WJ	Sheffield B	1931–77	Sheffield
WK	Coventry B	1926–63	Coventry A
		1949–75	Coventry B
WL	Oxford B	1926–74	Oxford
WM	Southport B	–	Presumed destroyed
WN	Swansea B	1927–48	Droitwich Spa
WO	Monmouthshire	1927–74	Cwmbran
WP	Worcestershire	1931–35	Worcester
		1931–48	Droitwich Spa
WR	Yorkshire (WR)	1921–37	Droitwich Spa
WS	Leith B	1903–20	Edinburgh
WT	Yorkshire (WR)	1921–37	Droitwich Spa
WU	Yorkshire (WR)	1921–37	Droitwich Spa
WV	Wiltshire	1931–74	Trowbridge
		1931–36	Bristol

		1937–48	Droitwich Spa
WW	Yorkshire (WR)	1936–37	Droitwich Spa
WX	Yorkshire (WR)	1929–37	Droitwich Spa
WY	Yorkshire (WR)	1921–37	Droitwich Spa
WZ	Belfast B	–	See Appendix 1
X	Northumberland	1903–21	Morpeth
XA	London/Kirkcaldy B[1]	–	Destroyed
XB	London/Coatbridge B	–	Destroyed
XC	London/Solihull B	–	Destroyed
XD	London/Luton B	–	Destroyed
XE	London/Luton B	–	Destroyed
XF	London	–	Destroyed
XF	Torbay	1968–76	Exeter B
XG	Middlesbrough B	1937–47	Middlesbrough
XH	London	–	Destroyed
XI	Belfast B	–	See Appendix 1
XJ	Manchester B	1968–74	Manchester B
XK	London	–	Destroyed
XL	London	–	Destroyed
XM	London	–	Destroyed
XN	London	–	Destroyed
XO	London	–	Destroyed
XP	London	–	Destroyed
XR	London ·	–	Destroyed
XS	Paisley B	1921–48	Droitwich Spa
XT	London	–	Destroyed
XU	London	–	Destroyed
XV	London	–	Destroyed
XW	London	–	Destroyed
XX	London	–	Destroyed
XY	London	–	Destroyed
XZ	Armagh	–	See Appendix 1

[1] This and subsequent marks used by London in the 1930s were reallocated in the 1960s as indicated, but only in the case of XF have any records survived.

Y	Somerset	1903–20	Taunton
		1903–20	Bristol
YA	Somerset	1921–71	Taunton
		1921–30	Bristol
YB	Somerset	1924–74	Taunton
		1924–30	Bristol
YC	Somerset	1927–71	Taunton
		1921–30	Bristol
YD	Somerset	1927–71	Taunton
YE	London	–	Destroyed
YF	London	–	Destroyed
YG	Yorkshire (WR)	1932–37	Droitwich Spa
YH	London	–	Destroyed
YI	Dublin B	1927–54	Dublin
YJ	Dublin B	1932–48	Dublin
YK	London	–	Destroyed
YL	London	–	Destroyed
YM	London	–	Destroyed
YN	London	–	Destroyed
YO	London	–	Destroyed
YP	London	–	Destroyed
YR	London	–	Destroyed
YS	Glasgow B	1935–48	Droitwich Spa
YT	London	–	Destroyed
YU	London	–	Destroyed
YV	London	–	Destroyed
YW	London	–	Destroyed
YX	London	–	Destroyed
YY	London	–	Destroyed
YZ	Londonderry	–	See Appendix 1

Z	Dublin County	1927–54	Dublin
ZA	Dublin B	1927–54	Dublin
ZB	Cork	1935–50	Cork A
ZC	Dublin B	1927–54	Dublin
ZD	Dublin B	1927–54	Dublin
ZE	Dublin B	1927–54	Dublin

ZF	Cork	1950–65	Cork A
		1966–87	Cork B
ZH	Dublin B	1927–54	Dublin
ZI	Dublin B	1927–54	Dublin
ZJ	Dublin B	1927–54	Dublin
ZK	Cork	1949–55	Cork A
ZL	Dublin	1927–54	Dublin
ZM	Galway	1950–87	Galway
ZN	Meath	1951–87	Navan
ZO	Dublin	1927–54	Dublin
ZP	Donegal	1921–87[1]	Letterkenny
ZR	Wexford	1921–87	Wexford
ZT	Cork	1953–55	Cork A
ZU	Dublin	1927–54	Dublin
ZW	Kildare	1953–87	Kildare B
ZX	Kerry	1954-87	Tralee
ZY	Louth	1954–87	Dundalk

[1] See note unde IH.

Where to find the Records

The following list gives full details of the record offices, libraries, museums and other locations at which the material described in the previous section is kept.

Aberystwyth
Ceredigion Archives, County Office, Marine Terrace, Aberystwyth SY23 2DE. Tel. 01920 633697.

Aylesbury
County Records and Local Studies Service, County Hall, Aylesbury, Bucks. HP20 1UU. Tel. 01926 382587. Fax 01296 382405.

Barrow-in-Furness
Cumbria Record Office, 140 Duke Street, Barrow-in-Furness LA14 1XW. Tel. 01229 894363. Fax 01229 894371.

Bedford
Bedfordshire & Luton Archives & Records Service, County Hall, Cauldwell Street, Bedford MK42 9AP. Tel. 01234 363222. Fax 01234 228854.

Belfast
Public Record Office of Northern Ireland, 66 Balmoral Avenue, Belfast BT9 6NY. Tel. 01232 251318. Fax 01232 255999.

Beverley
East Riding of Yorkshire Archive Office, County Hall, Beverley HU17 9BA. Tel. 01482 887700. Fax 01481 871277.

Birkenhead
The Archivist, Central Library, Borough Road, Birkenhead, Wirral L41 2XB. Tel. 0151 652 6106. Fax 0151 653 7320.

Birmingham
City Archives, Central Library, Chamberlain Square, Birmingham B3 3HQ. Tel. 0121 303 4217. Fax 0121 233 4458.

Bolton
Bolton Archive and Local Studies Service, Central Library, Civic Centre, Le Mans Crescent, Bolton BL1 1SE. Tel. 01204 522311 ext. 2179. Fax 01204 363224.

Bristol
Bristol Record Office, 'B' Bond Warehouse, Smeaton Road, Bristol BS1 6XN. Tel. 0117 922 5692. Fax 0117 922 4236.

Burton-upon-Trent
Burton Library, Riverside, High St, Burton-upon-Trent DE14 1AH. Tel. 01283 239556. Fax 01283 239571.

Bury St Edmunds
Bury St Edmunds Record Office, 77 Raingate Street, Bury St Edmunds, Suffolk IP33 2AR. Tel. 01284 352352. Fax 01284 352355.

Caernarfon
Caernarfon Record Office, Swyddfa'r Cyngor, Caernarfon, Gwynedd LL55 1SH. Tel. 01286 679088. Fax 01286 679637.

Cambridge
Cambridgeshire Heritage, Castle Court, Shire Hall, Castle Hill, Cambridge CB3 0AP. Tel. 01223 717281. Fax 01223 717201.

Canterbury
Cathedral Archives, The Precincts, Canterbury CT1 2EH. Tel. 01227 463510. Fax 01227 762897.

Cardiff A
Glamorgan Record Office, The Glamorgan Building, Cathays Park, Cardiff CF1 3NE. Tel. 01222 780282. Fax 01222 780284.

Cardiff B
Mr C.J. Taylor, 31 Heol Wen, Rhiwbina, Cardiff CF4 6EG. Tel. 01222 693734.

Carlisle
Cumbria Record Office, The Castle, Carlisle, Cumbria CA3 8UR. Tel. 01228 607285. Fax 01228 607299.

Carlow
County Library, Dublin St, Carlow, Co. Carlow, Ireland. Tel. 053 70300.

Carmarthen
Carmarthenshire Archives Service, County Hall, Carmarthen SA31 1JP. Tel. 01267 224184. Fax 01267 230848.

Carrick
Motor Registration Dept, Leitrim County Council, Park Lane House, Priest's Lane, Carrick-on-Shannon, Co. Leitrim, Ireland.

Castlebar
Motor Taxation Office, Mayo County Council, Castlebar, Mayo, Ireland.

Chelmsford
Essex Record Office, PO Box 11, County Hall, Chelmsford CM1 1LX. Tel. 01245 492211. Fax 01245 430085.

Chester A
Cheshire Record Office, Duke Street, Chester CH1 1RL. Tel. 01244 602559. Fax 01244 603812.

Chester B
Chester Archives, Town Hall, Chester CH1 2HJ. Tel. 01244 402110. Fax 01244 324338.

Chichester
West Sussex Record Office, County Hall, Chichester, West Sussex PO19 1RN. Tel. 01243 5333911. Fax 01243 533959.

Clonmel
Motor Taxation Office, Aras An Chontae, Emmet Street, Clonmel, Co. Tipperary, Ireland. Tel. 052 25399.

Cork A
Cork Archives Institute, Christ Church, South Main Street, Cork, Ireland. Tel. 021 277809.

Cork B
Motor Taxation Office, County Hall, Cork, Ireland. Tel. 021 544566. Fax 021 341007.

Coventry A
City Archives, Mandela House, Bayley Lane, Coventry CV1 5RG. Tel. 01203 832418. Fax 01203 832421.

Coventry B
Museum of British Road Transport, Hales Street, Coventry CV1 1PN. Tel. 01203 832425. Fax 01203 832465.

Cwmbran
Gwent Record Office, County Hall, Cwmbran, Gwent NP44 2XH. Tel. 01633 644888. Fax 01633 648382.

Dolgellau
Dolgellau Record Office, Cae Penarlâg, Dolgellau, Gwynedd LL40 2YB. Tel. 01341 424444. Fax 01341 423984.

Doncaster
Doncaster Archives, King Edward Road, Doncaster DN4 0NA. Tel. 01302 859811.

Dorchester
Dorset Record Office, Bridport Road, Dorchester DT1 1RP. Tel. 01305 250550. Fax 01305 257184.

Droitwich Spa
The Kithead Trust, De Salis Drive, Hampton Lovett, Droitwich Spa, Worcs. WR9 0QE. Tel. 01905 776681.

Dublin
Dublin City Archives, City Assembly House, 58 South William Street, Dublin 2, Ireland. Tel. 01 677 5877. Fax 01 677 5954.

Dudley
Archives and Local History Service, Mount Pleasant Street, Coseley, Dudley DY14 9JR. Tel. 01384 812770. Fax 01384 812770.

Dumfries
Dumfries and Galloway Archives, Archive Centre, 33 Burns Street, Dumfries DG1 2PS. Tel. 01387 269254. Fax 01387 264126.

Dundalk
Motor Taxation Dept, Louth County Council, Dundalk, Co. Louth, Ireland.

Dundee
Dundee City Archives, 21 City Square, Dundee DD1 3BY. Tel. 01382 434494. Fax 01382 434666.

Dungarvan
Motor Taxation Office, Waterford County Council, Shandon Road, Dungarvan, Co. Waterford, Ireland. Tel. 058 42822.

Durham
County Record Office, County Hall, Durham. Tel. 0191 383 4210. Fax 0191 383 4500.

Edinburgh
City Archives, City Chambers, High Street, Edinburgh EH1 1YJ. Tel. 0131 529 4093. Fax 0131 529 7477.

Elgin
Moray Heritage Officer, Moray Council, Grant Lodge, Elgin IV30 1HS. Tel. 01343 563413. Fax 01343 549050.

Ennis
Motor Taxation Office, Clare County Council, New Road, Ennis, Ireland. Tel. 065 21616.

Exeter A
Devon Record Office, Castle Street, Exeter EX4 3PU. Tel. 01392 384253. Fax 01392 384256.

Exeter B
Exeter Vehicle Registration Office, Hanover House, Manaton Close, Matford Business Park, Marsh Barton, Exeter EX2 8EF. Tel. 01392 270991. Fax 01392 431107.

Galway
Motor Taxation Dept, Galway County Council, Galway, Ireland.

Glasgow
Glasgow City Archives, The Mitchell Library, 201 North Street, Glasgow G3 7DN. Tel. 0141 287 2913. Fax 0141 226 8452.

Gloucester
County Record Office, Clarence Row, Alvin Street, Gloucester GL1 3DW. Tel. 01452 425295. Fax 01452 426378.

Grimsby
North East Lincolnshire Archives, Town Hall, Town Hall Square, Grimsby DN31 1HZ. Tel. 01472 323585.

Halifax
West Yorkshire Archive Service, Central Library, Northgate House, Northgate, Halifax HX1 1UN. Tel. 01422 392636. Fax 01422 341083.

Haverfordwest
Pembrokeshire Record Office, The Castle, Haverfordwest, Pembrokeshire SA61 2EF. Tel. 01437 763707.

Hawarden
County Record Office, The Old Rectory, Hawarden CH5 3NR. Tel. 01244 532364. Fax 01244 538344.

Hawick
Hawick Museum, Wilton Lodge, Hawick TD9 7JL. Tel. 01450 373457. Fax 01450 378526.

Hereford
Record Office, The Old Barracks, Harold Street, Hereford HR1 2QX. Tel. 01432 265441. Fax 01432 370248.

Hertford
Archives and Local Studies, County Hall, Hertford SG13 8EJ. Tel. 01992 555105. Fax 01992 555113.

Holywood
Ulster Folk and Transport Museum, Cultra, Holywood, Co. Down, Northern Ireland BT18 0EU. Tel. 01232 428428. Fax 01232 428728.

Hull A
Hull Archives, 79 Lowgate, Hull HU1 2HN. Tel. 01482 613902. Fax 01482 613710.

Hull B
Hull Museum of Museum, High Street, Hull HU1 1NQ. Tel. 01482 613902. Fax 01482 613710.

Huntingdon
County Record Office, Grammar School Walk, Huntingdon PE18 6LF. Tel. 01480 375842. Fax 01480 459563.

Inverness
Highland Council Archive, Farraline Park, Inverness IV1 1NH. Tel. 01463 220330. Fax 01463 711128.

Ipswich
Ipswich Record Office, Gatacre Road, Ipswich IP1 2LQ. Tel. 01473 584541. Fax 01473 584533.

Kendal
Cumbria Record Office, County Offices, Kendal, Cumbria LA9 4RQ. Tel. 01539 773540. Fax 01539 773439.

Kilkenny
County Library, 6 John's Quay, Kilkenny, Ireland. Tel. 056 22021. Fax 056 63384.

Kirkwall
Orkney Library, Laing Street, Kirkwall, Orkney KW15 1NW. Tel. 01856 873166. Fax 01856 875260.

Leicester
Leicestershire Record Office, Long Street, Wigston Magna, Leicester LE18 2AH. Tel. 0116 257 1020. Fax 0116 257 1120.

Leigh
Wigan Archives Service, Town Hall, Leigh WN7 2DY. Tel. 01942 404430. Fax 01942 404505.

Leigh-on-Sea
Mr J. Taylor, 113 Beach Avenue, Leigh-on-Sea, Essex SS9 1HD. Tel. 01702 478000.

Letterkenny
County Library, Letterkenny, Co. Donegal, Ireland Tel. 074 21968. Fax 074 26402.

Lerwick
Shetland Archives, King Harald Street, Lerwick, Shetland ZE1 0EQ. Tel. 01595 3535. Fax 01595 696533.

Lewes
East Sussex Record Office, The Maltings, Castle Precincts, Lewes, East Sussex BN7 1YT. Tel. 01273 482349. Fax 01273 482341.

Limerick A
Limerick Regional Archives, The Granary, Michael Street, Limerick, Ireland. Tel. 061 410777. Fax 061 415215.

Limerick B
Motor Taxation Department, Limerick County Council, O'Connell Street, Limerick, Ireland.

Lincoln
Lincolnshire Archives, St Rumbold Street, Lincoln LN2 5AB. Tel. 01523 525158. Fax 01523 530047.

Llandrindod Wells
County Archives Office, County Hall, Llandrindod Wells LD1 5LG. Tel. 01597 826087. Fax 01597 826230.

Llangefni
Anglesey County Record Office, Shirehll, Glanhwfa Road, Llangefni, Anglesey LL77 7TW. Tel. 01248 752080. Fax 01248 750365.

Lochgilphead
The Archivist, Corporate Services, Argyll and Bute Council, Kilmory, Lochgilphead, Argyll PA31 8RT. Tel. 01546 602127. Fax 01546 604138.

London
London Metropolitan Archives, 40 Northampton Road, London EC1R 0HB. Tel. 0171 332 3820. Fax 0171 833 9136.

Longford
Motor Taxation Office, Longford County Council, Great Water Street, Longford, Co. Longford, Ireland. Tel. 043 46231.

Loughborough
Mr J. Bennett, 174 Leicester Road, Loughborough, Leics. LE11 2AH. Tel. 01509 263601.

Maidstone
Centre for Kentish Studies, County Hall, Maidstone ME14 1XQ. Tel. 01622 694363. Fax 01622 694379.

Manchester A
Greater Manchester Record Office, 56 Marshall Street, New Cross, Manchester M4 5FU. Tel. 0161 832 5284. Fax 0161 839 3808.

Manchester B
Archives Dept, Central Library, St Peter's Square, Manchester M2 5PD. Tel. 0161 234 1980. Fax 0161 234 1927.

Matlock
Derbyshire Record Office, County Hall, Matlock, Derbyshire DE4 3AG. Tel. 01629 580000. Fax 01629 57611.

Middlesbrough
Cleveland Archives, Exchange House, 6 Marton Road, Middlesbrough TS1 1DB. Tel. 01642 248321.

Monaghan
Motor Tax Office, Monaghan County Council, County Offices, The Glen, Monaghan, Ireland. Tel. 047 82211.

Morpeth
Morpeth Records Centre, The Lylins, Loansdean, Morpeth NE71 2EQ. Tel. 01670 504084.

Navan
Motor Taxation Dept, Meath County Council, County Hall, Navan, Co. Meath, Ireland. Tel. 046 21581. Fax 046 21463.

Nenagh
Motor Taxation Office, Tipperary (NR) County Council, Kickham Street, Nenagh, Ireland. Tel. 067 31771.

Newbridge A
County Library, Newbridge, Co. Kildare, Ireland. Tel. 045 31486/31109.

Newbridge B
Motor Taxation Office, Kildare County Council, Newbridge, Co. Kildare, Ireland.

Northallerton
County Record Office, County Hall, Northallerton DL7 8AF. Tel. 01609 777585. Fax 01609 777078.

Northampton
Northamptonshire Record Office, Wootton Hall Park, Northampton NN4 8BQ. Tel. 01604 762129. Fax 01604 767562.

Norwich
Norfolk Record Office, Gildengate House, Anglia Square, Upper Green Lane, Norwich NR3 1AX. Tel. 01603 761349. Fax 01603 761885.

Nottingham A
Nottinghamshire Archives, County House, Castle Meadow Road, Nottingham NG2 1AG. Tel. 0115 958 1634. Fax 0115 941 3997.

Nottingham B
Mr R.G. Westgate, 243 Oakdale Road, Carlton, Nottingham NG4 1AA.

Oldham
Archive Service, Local Studies Library, 84 Union Street, Oldham OL1 1DN. Tel. 0161 911 4654. Fax 0161 911 4669.

Oxford
Oxfordshire Archives, County Hall, New Road, Oxford OX1 1ND. Tel. 01865 815203. Fax 01865 810187.

Plymouth
Plymouth & West Devon Record Office, Unit 3, Clare Place, Coxside, Plymouth PL4 0JW. Tel. 01752 305940. Fax 01752 223939.

Polegate
Filching Manor Motor Museum, Wannock, Polegate, Sussex BN26 5QA. Tel. 01323 487838. Fax 01323 486331.

Portlaoise
Motor Taxation Dept, Laois County County, County Hall, Portlaoise, Co. Laois, Ireland. Tel. 0502 22044.

Preston
Lancashire Record Office, Bow Lane, Preston PR1 2RE. Tel. 01772 263034. Fax 01772 263050.

Reading
Berkshire Record Office, Shinfield Park, Reading RG2 9XD. Tel. 0118 923 3182. Fax 0118 923 3181.

Roscommon
Motor Taxation Office, Roscommon County Council, Roscommon, Ireland. Tel. 903 26100.

Ruthin
Denbighshire Record Office, 46 Clwyd Street, Ruthin, Denbighshire LL15 1HP. Tel. 01824 703077. Fax 01824 705180.

St Helens
Local History and Archives Library, The Gamble Building, Victoria Square, St Helens, Merseyside WA10 1DY. Tel. 01744 456952. Fax 01744 20836.

Salford
Archives Centre, 658-662 Liverpool Road, Irlam, Salford M44 5AD. Tel. 0161 775 5463.

Sheffield
Sheffield Archives, 52 Shoreham Street, Sheffield S1 4SP. Tel. 0114 203 9395. Fax 0114 203 9398.

Shrewsbury
Shropshire Records and Research Service, Castle Gates, Shrewsbury SY1 1AQ. Tel. 01743 255350. Fax 01743 255355.

Sligo A
County Library Headquarters, The Westward Town Centre, Bridge Street, Sligo, Ireland. Tel. 071 47190. Fax 071 467798

Sligo B
Motor Tax Office, Cleveragh Road, Sligo, Ireland.

Smethwick
Community History and Archives Service, Smethwick Library, High Street, Smethwick, Warley B66 1AB. Tel. 0121 558 2561. Fax 0121 555 6064.

Southampton
Archive Services, Civic Centre, Southampton SO14 7LY. Tel. 01703 223855. Fax 01703 336305.

Southend
Essex Record Office, Southend Branch, Central Library, Victoria Avenue, Southend-on-Sea SS2 6EX. Tel. 01702 464278. Fax 01702 464523.

Stafford
Staffordshire Record Office, Eastgate Street, Stafford ST16 2LZ. Tel. 01785 278379. Fax 01785 278384.

Stirling
Stirling Council Archives, Unit 6, Burghmuir Industrial Estate, Stirling FK7 7PY. Tel. O1786 450745.

Stoke-on-Trent
Stoke-on-Trent City Archives, Hanley Library, Bethesda Street, Hanley, Stoke-on-Trent ST1 3RS. Tel. 01782 238420.

Stranraer
Stranraer Museum, 55 George Street, Stranraer DG9 7JP. Tel. 01776 705088. Fax 01776 704420.

Swansea
West Glamorgan Archive Service, County Hall, Oystermouth Road, Swansea SA1 3SN. Tel. 01792 636589. Fax 01792 636340.

Taunton
Somerset Record Office, Obridge Road, Taunton TA2 7PU. Tel. 01823 278805. Fax 01823 325402.

Tralee
Motor Taxation Dept, Kerry County Council, Moyderwell, Tralee, Co. Kerry, Ireland. Tel. 066 22300.

Trowbridge
Wiltshire Record Office, County Hall, Trowbridge, Wilts. BA14 8JG. Tel. 01225 713139. Fax 01225 713999.

Truro
Cornwall Record Office, County Hall, Truro TR1 3AY. Tel. 01872 73698.

Tullamore
County Library, O'Connor Square, Tullamore, Co. Offaly, Ireland. Tel. 0506 46834. Fax 0506 52769.

Wakefield
West Yorkshire Archive Service, Registry of Deeds, Newstead Road, Wakefield WF1 2DE. Tel. 01924 305980. Fax 01924 305983.

Walsall
Local History Centre, Essex Street, Walsall WS2 7AS. Tel. 01922 721305. Fax 01922 634954.

Warrington
Mr A.R. Phillips, 16 Victoria Avenue, Grappenhall, Warrington WA4 2PD.

Warwick
County Record Office, Priory Park, Cape Road, Warwick CV34 4JS. Tel. 01926 412735. Fax 01926 412509.

Waterford
Motor Taxation Office, Waterford Corporation, Waterford, Ireland. Tel. 051 873501.

Wexford
Motor Taxation Dept, County Hall, Wexford, Ireland.

Wicklow
Motor Taxation Dept, Wicklow County Council, Wicklow, Ireland.

Winchester
Hampshire Record Office, Sussex Street, Winchester SO23 8TH. Tel. 01962 846154. Fax 01962 878681.

Wolverhampton
Wolverhampton Archives and Local Studies, 42–50 Snow Hill, Wolverhampton WV2 4AG. Tel. 01902 552480. Fax 01902 552481.

Worcester
Record Office, County Hall, Spetchley Road, Worcester WR5 2NP. Tel. 01905 766352. Fax 01905 766363.

York
City Archives, Art Gallery Building,
Exhibition Square, York YO1 2EW.
Tel. 01904 551878. Fax 01904
551877.

Motor Museums

The following list includes museums in the British Isles devoted entirely to motoring, plus transport museums with substantial road vehicle collections. As well as providing an enjoyable day out for anyone interested in the history of motoring, many of the museums listed here will be able to offer advice and information on the history of particular cars and other vehicles. The help of the National Motor Museum, Beaulieu, in compiling this list is gratefully acknowledged.

ENGLAND

Batley
Skopos Motor Museum, Alexandra Mills, Alexandra Road, Batley, W. Yorks. WF17 6JA. Tel. 01924 444423. Fax 01924 422124.

Battlesbridge
Battlesbridge Motorcycle Museum, Muggeridge Farm, Battlesbridge, Essex SS11 7RF. Tel. 01268 769392.

Beaulieu
National Motor Museum, John Montagu Building, Beaulieu, Brockenhurst, Hants. SO42 7ZN. Tel. 01590 612345. Fax 01590 612655.

Benfleet
Castle Point Transport Museum, 5 Barncombe Close, Thundersley, Benfleet, Essex.

Beverley
Museum of Army Transport, Flemingate, Beverley HU17 0NG. Tel. 01482 860445. Fax 01482 872767.

Birkenhead
Birkenhead Transport Museum, Tram Shed, Pacific Road, Birkenhead, Wirral. Tel. and fax 0151 666 2756.

Birmingham
Aston Manor Road Transport Museum, The Old Tram Depot, 208-216 Witton Lane, Aston, Birmingham. Tel. 0121 322 2298.

Birmingham and Midland Museum of Transport, Chapel Lane, Wythall, Birmingham B47 6JX. Tel. 01564 826471. Fax 01564 826666.

Bournemouth
Bournemouth Transport Museum, Building 101, N.W. Industrial Estate, Bournemouth Airport, Christchurch

BH23 6NW. Tel. 01202 590026.

Bourton-on-the-Water
Costwold Motor Museum, The Old Mill, Bourton-on-the-Water, Gloucs. GL54 2BY. Tel. 01451 821255.

Bovington
The Tank Museum, Bovington Camp, Wareham, Dorset BH20 6JG. Tel. 01929 405096. Fax 01929 405360.

Bradford
West Yorkshire Transport Trust, Ludlam Street, Mill Lane, Off Manchester Road, Bradford BD5 0HG

Transperience Discovery Park, Transperience Way, Bradford BD12 7HQ. Tel. 01274 690909. Fax 01274 693651.

Brentford
Heritage Motor Museum, Syon Park, Brentford, Middlesex TW8 8JF

Bridgnorth
Midland Motor Museum, Stanmore Hall, Stourbridge Road, Bridgnorth, Shropshire WV15 6DT. Tel. 01746 762992. Fax 01746 768104.

Bury
Bury Transport Museum, Bolton Street Station, Bolton Street, Bury, Lancs. BL9 0EY

Caister-on-Sea
Caister Castle Motor Museum, Caister-on-Sea, Great Yarmouth, Norfolk. Tel. 01572 787251. Fax 01572 787473.

Calne
Atwell-Wilson Motor Museum, Downside, Stockley Lane, Calne, Wilts. SN11 0NF. Tel. 01249 813119.

Canterbury
Canterbury Motor Museum, 11 Cogans Terrace, Canterbury CT1 3SJ. Tel. 01227 464272.

Canvey Island
Castle Point Transport Museum, 105 Point Road, Canvey Island, Essex SS8 7TP. Tel. 01268 684272.

Cark-in-Cartmel
Lakeland Motor Museum, Holker Hall, Cark-in-Cartmel, Cumbria LA11 7PL. Tel. 01539 558509.

Castle Donington
Donington Grand Prix Collection, Donington Park, Castle Donington, Derby DE7 2RP. Tel. 01332 811027. Fax 01332 812829.

Chumleigh
West of England Transport Collection, 15 Land Park, Chumleigh, N. Devon EX18 7BH.

Cobham
Cobham Bus Museum, Redhill Road, Cobham, Surrey KT11 1EF. Tel. 01932 864078. Fax 01932 057660.

Cockermouth
Cockermouth Motor Museum, The Maltings, Brewery Lane, Cockermouth, Cumbria CA13 9NE. Tel. 01900 824448.

Combe Martin
Combe Martin Motorcycle Collection, Cross Street, Combe Martin, N. Devon EX34 0DH. Tel. 01271 882346.

Coventry
Museum of British Road Transport, Hales Street, Coventry CV1 1PN. Tel. 01203 832425. Fax 01203 832465.

Jaguar Daimler Heritage Trust, Browns Lane, Allesley, Coventry CV4 9DR. Tel. 01203 402121. Fax 01203 405581.

Dover
Dover Transport Museum, Old Park, Whitfield, Dover. Tel. 01304 204612.

Dunsfold
Dunsfold Land Rovers Ltd, Alford Road, Dunsfold, Godalming, Surrey GU8 4NP. Tel. 01483 200567. Fax 01483 200738.

Fleetwood
All American Automobile Show, Fleetwood Freeport, Anchorage Road, Fleetwood, Lancs. FY7 6AE. Tel. 01345 697016.

Frodsham
Mouldsworth Motor Museum, The Balcony House, Erindale Crescent, Frodsham, Cheshire WA6 6DZ. Tel. 01923 731781.

Gateshead
North East Bus Museum, Leam Lane, Wardley, Gateshead NE10 8YY. Tel. 01670 828034. Fax 01670 027961.

Gaydon
Heritage Motor Centre, Banbury Road, Gaydon, Warwick CV35 0BJ. Tel. 01926 641188. Fax 01926 641555.

Gloucester
Gloucester Transport Museum, The Old Fire Station, Bearland, Gloucs. Tel. 01452 526467.

Gotherington
The Bugatti Trust, Prescott, Gotherington, Cheltenham, Gloucs. GL52 4RD. Tel. 01242 677201. Fax 01242 674191.

Guildford
The A.R.E. Classic Bike Collecton, 285 Wordlesdon Road, Guildford, Surrey. Tel. and fax 01483 232006.

Halland
Bentley Wildfowl and Motor Museum, Halland, Lewes, Sussex BN8 4AF. Tel. 01825 840573.

Halifax
Meltham Mills Bus Museum, 1 Vicar Park Road, Norton Tower, Halifax HX2 0NL. Tel. 01422 343557.

Hebden Bridge
Autombobilia Transport Museum, Billy Lane, Old Town, Hebden Bridge, W. Yorks. HX7 8RY.

High Wycombe
Dewsbury Bus Museum, 1a Barberswood Close, High Wycombe, Bucks. HP12 4EW. Tel. 01494 521994.

Huddersfield
Automobilia, The Heritage Centre, Leeds Road, Huddersfield HD1 6QA. Tel. and fax 01484 559092.

Hull
Streetlife: Hull Museum of Transport, High Street, Hull HU1 1NQ. Tel. 01482 613902. Fax 01482 613710.

Ipswich
Ipswich Transport Museum, Old Trolleybus Depot, Cobham Road, Ipswich IP3 9JD. Tel. 01473 715666. Fax 01473 832260.

Keighley
Keighley Bus Museum, Denholme House Farm, Denholme, Bradford, W. Yorks. Tel. 01282 413179.

Keswick
Cars of the Stars Motor Museum, Standish Street, Keswick, Cumbria CA12 5LS. Tel. 01768 773757. Fax 01768 772810.

Kings Norton
The Patrick Collection, 180 Lifford Lane, Kings Norton, Birmingham B30 3NT.

Leyland
British Commercial Vehicle Museum, King Street, Leyland, Preston PR5 1LE. Tel. 01772 451011. Fax 01772 623404.

London
London Transport Museum, 39 Wellington Street, Covent Garden, London WC2E 7BB. Tel. 0171 379 6344.

Fax 0171 836 4118.

Long Hanborough
Oxford Bus Museum, Long Hanborough, Woodstock, Oxon. Tel. 01993 883617.

Lowestoft
East Anglia Transport Museum, Chapel Colville, Carlton Road, Lowestoft, Suffolk NR33 8BL. Tel. 01502 518459.

Lutterworth
Stanford Hall Motorcycle Museum, Lutterworth, Leics. LE17 6DH. Tel. 01788 860250. Fax 01788 860870.

Manchester
Manchester Transport Museum, 412 King's Road, Ashton-under-Lyne, Lancs. OL6 9AT.

Manchester Museum of Transport, Boyle Street, Cheetham, Manchester M8 8UL. Tel. 0161 205 1082. Fax 0161 205 2122.

Mouldsworth
Mouldworth Motor Museum, Smithy Lane, Mouldworth, Cheshire CH3 8AR. Tel. 01928 731781.

Newburn
Newburn Hall Motor Museum, 35 Townfield Gardens, Newburn, Tyne & Wear NE15 8PY. Tel. 0191 264 2977.

New Milton
Sammy Miller Motorcyle Museum, Bashley Manor Farm, Bashley Cross Roads, New Milton, Hants. BH25

5SJ. Tel. 01425 616644.

North Hykeham
Lincolnshire Road Transport Museum, Whisby Road, North Hykeham, Lincs. LN6 3QT. Tel. 01522 500566.

Polegate
Filching Manor Motor Museum, Wannock, Polegate, Sussex BN26 5QA. Tel. 01323 487838. Fax 01323 486331.

Portsmouth
City of Portsmouth Preserved Transport Depot, 48–54 Broad Street, Old Portsmouth, Hants. Tel. and fax 01705 363478.

Ramsgate
Ramsgate Motor Museum, Westcliff Hall, Ramsgate, Kent CT11 9JX. Tel. 01843 581948.

Rolvenden
C.M. Booth Collection of Historic Vehicles, 63–67 High Street, Rolvenden, Cranbrook, Kent TN17 4LP. Tel. 01580 241234.

St Austell
Automobilia, The Old Mill, St Stephen, St Austell, Cornwall. Tel. 01726 823092.

St Helens
St Helens Transport Museum, Old Bus Depot, 51 Hall Street, St Helens WA10 1DU. Tel. 01744 451681.

Sheffield
Sheffield Bus Museum, Tinsley Tramsheds, Sheffield Road, Sheffield. Tel. 0114 255 3010.

Sidmouth
Motoring Memories, Old Fire Station, High Street, Sidmouth, Devon EX10 8EF. Tel. 01297 552341.

Solihull
National Motorcycle Museum, Coventry Road, Bickenhill, Solihull B92 0EJ. Tel. 01675 443311. Fax 01675 443310.

South Witham
Geeson Bros. Motorcycle Museum and Workshop, 6 Water Lane, South Witham, Grantham, Lincs. NG33 5H. Tel. 01572 767280.

Sparkford
Haynes Motor Museum, Sparkford, Yeovil, Somerset BA22 7LH. Tel. 01963 440804. Fax 01963 440023.

Stockon-on-the-Forest
The Craven Collection of Classic Motorcyles, Brockfield Villa, Stockton-on-the-Forest, York YO3 9UE. Tel. 01904 488461.

Straford-upon-Avon
Stratford Motor Museum, 1 Shakespeare Street, Stratford-upon-Avon, Warwickshire.

Tavistock
National Ambulance Museum, Half Bridge, Tavistock, Devon PL19 9LR.

Thornton-le-Dale
North Yorkshire Motor Museum, Roxby Garage, Pickering Road, Thornton-le-Dale, N. Yorks. YO18 4LH. Tel. 01751 474455.

Totnes
Totnes Motor Museum, Steamer Quay, Totnes, Devon TQ9 5AL.

Ulverston
Phil Cotton's Classic Motorcycles, Victoria Road, Ulverston, Cumbria LA12 0BY. Tel. 01229 586099. Fax 01229 586399.

Weston-super-Mare
Weston-super-Mare Motoring and Memorabilia Museum, 4 Chestnut Chase, Nailsea BS19 1QB. Tel. 01275 857855.

Weybridge
Brooklands Museum, The Clubhouse, Brooklands Road, Weybridge, Surrey KT13 0QN. Tel. 01932 857381. Fax 01932 855465.

Windsor
History on Wheels Museum, Longclose House, Little Common Road, Eton Wick, Windsor, Berks. SL4 6QY. Tel. 01753 862637. Fax 01753 841998.

SCOTLAND

Aberlady
Myreton Motor Museum, Aberlady, East Lothian EH32 0PZ. Tel. 01875 870288.

Alexandria
Classic Car Collection, Motor Heritage Centre, Loch Lomond Outlets, The Argyll Building, Main Street, Alexandria G83 0UG. Tel. and fax 01389 607862.

Alford
Grampian Transport Museum, Alford, Aberdeenshire AB33 8AD. Tel. 01975 562292. Fax 01975 562180.

Biggar
Biggar Museum Trust, Gladstone Court Museum, Lanarkshire ML12 6DT. Tel. 01899 221050.

Doune
Doune Motor Museum, Carse of Cambus, Doune, Perthshire FK16 6HD. Tel. 01786 841203. Fax 01786 842070.

Elgin
Moray Motor Museum, Bridge Street, Bishopmill, Elgin, Morayshire IV30 2DE. Tel. 01343 544933.

Glasgow
Museum of Transport, Kelvin Hall, 1 Bunhouse Road, Glasgow G3 8DP. Tel. 0141 221 9600.

Glenluce
Glenluce Motor Museum, Glenluce, Wigtonshire DG8 0NY. Tel. 01581 300534.

Lathalmond
Scottish Vintage Bus Museum, Dunfermline, Fife. Tel. 01383 623380.

Melrose
Melrose Motor Museum, Annay Road, Melrose, Roxburghshire TD6 9LW.

WALES

Betws-y-coed
Betws-y-coed Motor Museum, Betwsy-coed, Gwynedd LL24 0AH. Tel. 01690 710760.

Haverfordwest
Pembrokeshire Motor Museum, Keeston Hill, Haverfordwest, Pembs. SA62 6EJ. Tel. 01437 710950.

Llangollen
Llangollen Motor Museum, Pentrefelin, Llangollen LL20 8EE. Tel. 01978 860324.

Porthmadog
Madog Motor Museum, Porthmadog, Gwynedd. Tel. 01758 712308.

NORTHERN IRELAND

Ulster Folk and Transport Museum, Cultra, Holywood BT18 0EU. Tel. 01232 428428. Fax 01232 428728.

REPUBLIC OF IRELAND

National Museum of Irish Transport, Scotts Garden, Killarney, Co. Kerry. Tel. 064 34677. Fax 064 31582.

National Transport Museum, Howth Castle Demesne, Howth, Co. Dublin. Tel. 01 848 0831.

CHANNEL ISLANDS

Jersey Motor Museum, St Peter's Village, Jersey, Channel Islands JE3 7AG. Tel. 01534 482966.

ISLE OF MAN

Manx Motor Museum, Crosby, Isle of Man. Tel. 01624 851236.

Murray's Motorcycle Museum, Bungalow Corner, TT Course, Snaefell Mountain, Isle of Man. Tel. 01624 861719.